MANITOBA
WAYSIDE
WILDFLOWERS

Linda Kershaw

Lone Pine Publishing

The Publisher: Lone Pine Publishing

10145 – 81 Avenue   1808 – B Street NW, Suite 140
Edmonton, AB, Canada T6E 1W9   Auburn, WA, USA 98001

Website: www.lonepinepublishing.com

National Library of Canada Cataloguing in Publication Data

Kershaw, Linda J., 1951–
  Manitoba wayside wildflowers / Linda Kershaw.

  Includes bibliographical references and index.
  ISBN 1-55105-352-7

  1. Wild flowers—Manitoba—Identification. I. Title.
QK203.M3K47 2003   582.13'097127   C2002-910728-8

Editorial Director: Nancy Foulds
Project Editor: Dawn Loewen
Illustrations Coordinator: Carol Woo
Production Coordinator: Jennifer Fafard
Book Design: Heather Markham
Layout & Production: Heather Markham, Lynett McKell
Cover Design: Gerry Dotto
Botanical Illustrations: Linda Kershaw
Scanning, Separations & Film: Elite Lithographers Co.

All other photographs by Linda Kershaw except the following, reproduced with the generous permission of their copyright holders: Lorna Allen, 37b, 39a, 63a&b, 139b; Terry Clayton, 120a&b, 125b, 139a; Robert Frisch, 118a

DISCLAIMER: This book is not meant to be a 'how-to' guide for using plants. We do not recommend experimentation by readers, and we caution that many plants, including some traditional medicines, are poisonous or otherwise harmful. Self-medication with herbs is unwise, and wild plant foods should be used with caution and expert advice.

We acknowledge the financial support of the Government of Canada through the Book Publishing Industry Development Program (BPIDP) for our publishing activities.

PC: P1

Contents

The wildflowers in this guide, arranged by flower colour

great blanketflower
p. 74

scarlet globe-mallow
p. 123

orange hawkweed
p. 68

wood lily
p. 113

black-eyed Susan
p. 73

greater bladderwort
p. 39

yellow lady's-slipper
p. 36

common tansy
p. 85

bird's-foot-trefoil
p. 49

annual sunflower
p. 72

marsh ragwort
p. 83

perennial sow-thistle
p. 69

common dandelion
p. 70

hairy false-golden-aster
p. 75

yellow pond-lily
p. 114

wild parsnip
p. 95

sweet-clover
p. 53

Canada goldenrod
p. 90

common silverweed
p. 127

meadow buttercup
p. 116

curly-cup gumweed
p. 76

narrow-leaved hawkweed
p. 67

butter-and-eggs
p. 38

fringed yellow-loosestrife
p. 124

annual hawk's-beard
p. 66

yellow marsh-marigold
p. 115

plains cinquefoil
p. 128

yellow avens
p. 126

shrubby cinquefoil
p. 130

tumbleweed mustard
p. 106

wormseed wallflower
p. 105

heart-leaved Alexanders
p. 96

common goat's-beard
p. 71

prickly lettuce
p. 65

wild mustard
p. 107

golden corydalis
p. 37

common evening-primrose
p. 137

leafy spurge
p. 91

pineappleweed
p. 86

curly dock
p. 103

common pepper-grass
p. 104

American licorice
p. 50

late yellow locoweed
p. 51

tall meadow-rue
p. 102

northern bedstraw
p. 100

white death-camas
p. 112

white cinquefoil
p. 129

cream-coloured vetchling
p. 48

little-leaved pussytoes
p. 87

starry false-
Solomon's-seal, p. 111

prairie onion
p. 97

northern grass-of-
Parnassus, p. 119

water calla
p. 58

common cow-parsnip
p. 92

arctic sweet-colt's-foot
p. 84

common yarrow
p. 89

buck-bean
p. 108

Canada anemone
p. 117

Virginia strawberry
p. 132

false-toadflax
p. 98

oxeye daisy
p. 77

scentless chamomile
p. 78

rusty Labrador-tea
p. 139

bunchberry
p. 59

field mouse-ear-
chickweed, p. 121

arum-leaved arrowhead
p. 109

Canada violet
p. 44

spotted water-hemlock
p. 94

common water-parsnip
p. 93

hedge false-bindweed
p. 147

long-leaved bluets
p. 99

scarlet butterflyweed
p. 138

smooth fleabane
p. 81

alsike clover
p. 55

bladder campion
p. 122

brittle-stem hemp-nettle
p. 42

spreading dogbane
p. 142

field bindweed
p. 146

northern crane's-bill
p. 133

Canada thistle
p. 61

lesser burdock
p. 60

Philadelphia fleabane
p. 82

beeplant
p. 120

common milkweed
p. 141

showy milkweed
p. 140

veiny vetchling
p. 47

hairy hedge-nettle
p. 41

water smartweed
p. 57

spotted Joe-Pye weed
p. 88

prickly rose
p. 131

American sweet-vetch
p. 45

wild bergamot
p. 40

dotted blazingstar
p. 63

common fireweed
p. 136

red clover
p. 56

purple loosestrife
p. 135

nodding plumeless-thistle
p. 62

showy locoweed
p. 52

three-flowered avens
p. 125

prairie-crocus
p. 118

early blue violet
p. 43

alfalfa
p. 54

American vetch
p. 46

smooth blue
American-aster, p. 80

fringed American-aster
p. 79

common blue lettuce
p. 64

harebell
p. 145

tall bluebells
p. 144

common blue-eyed-grass
p. 110

blue giant-hyssop
p. 101

common viper's-bugloss
p. 143

wild blue flax
p. 134

Why Learn More About Wildflowers?

Imagine a summer without wildflowers: an endless monotony of brown, grey and green. Instead of that boring scene, our eyes are treated to yellows, oranges, pinks, whites and purples, a colourful patchwork that changes throughout the summer. Wildflowers add beauty and variety to the roads, streets, sidewalks and pathways that crisscross our countryside.

But wayside wildflowers provide much more than simple decoration. Many of these hardy plants are important to the ecology of disturbed areas such as roadsides and vacant lots. At first, newly cleared areas are simply bare soil, usually with lots of rocks, low fertility and a tendency to wash away in the rain. Only the toughest plants can tolerate such harsh conditions. Those that do survive help make the soil more fertile for other plants and help hold the soil so it isn't swept away by wind and water. Common wildflowers also provide food and shelter for lots of different animals.

Many wildflowers have fascinating histories that extend back for centuries. Local Native peoples used many of these plants for food and medicine long before settlers arrived from Europe. Almost one-third of the plants in this guide, however, were brought to North America from Europe and Asia. Some arrived as valued garden plants, but others sneaked in with livestock and crop seed. Nowadays, some of the species in this guide are considered weeds— unwanted but highly successful plants that can choke out crops and gardens (see p. 14). Still, to the casual passerby, they remain beautiful wildflowers, blanketing waysides with a mosaic of colours and textures.

It's fun to get to know wildflowers by name. Just as recognizing your friends Judy, Roy and Inger means much more than seeing a group of strangers, recognizing prairie-crocus, black-eyed Susan and bird's-foot-trefoil means more than simply seeing 'some plants.' Once you know what to look for, it's easy to see the differences between wildflowers and to learn their names. Getting to know common flowers gives us a glimpse of the great variety of life around us, even in roadside ditches.

Black-eyed Susan and other flowers brighten many Manitoba roadsides.

What Is a Wildflower?

Most of us enjoy all sorts of flowers through the year and recognize many different types, from tulips in our gardens, to carnations at the florist's, to dandelions growing wild. But what exactly is a flower, and why do plants produce such an amazing array of showy, colourful blooms?

The main function of a flower is to produce seed so that the plant can leave offspring, spread to new areas and increase in number. Technically, a flower is a shortened shoot with a compact cluster of leaves that have been modified into specialized structures (such as petals) for reproduction. Most of the wildflowers in this guide have *perfect* flowers, with both male and female parts, but some species have male flowers on one plant and female flowers on another. The illustration on this page shows a cross-section of a typical perfect flower.

Let's start with the most important parts: the male and female structures.

The male part of the typical flower is the *stamen*. Often a flower has many stamens, each consisting of a slender stalk called a *filament* tipped with a round to oblong body called an *anther*. The anther contains many tiny grains of *pollen*, which usually look like yellow powder. Each microscopic grain contains one sperm cell that carries half the plant's genes.

The female part of the flower is the *pistil*. Often a flower has just one pistil, but it may have many, and they may be fused. Each pistil has three main parts: the *stigma* at the tip, designed to catch pollen grains; the stalk or *style* in the middle; and the *ovary* at the base. The ovary contains one to many *ovules*, each with an egg cell that carries half the plant's genes. An ovule becomes a *seed* when its egg cell is fertilized by a sperm cell. At the same time, the ovary surrounding the seed or seeds matures into a *fruit*. Fruits come in many forms, including fleshy berries, hard nutlets and pea-like pods.

The nonsexual parts of a flower help ensure successful *pollination*, which is the transfer of pollen from an anther to a stigma. A typical flower has two rings of structures surrounding its male and female parts. The outermost structure, the *calyx*, is made up of separate or fused *sepals*, which are usually green and leaf-like.

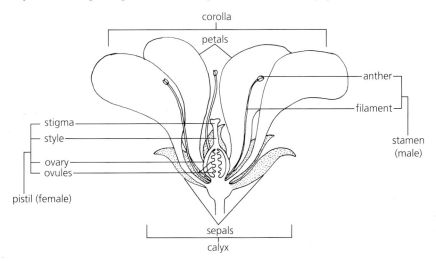

Sepals cover developing flower buds; they may also shelter mature flower parts and eventually protect the seeds. Within the calyx is the *corolla*, made up of separate or fused *petals*. Most of the colourful structures that we see in wildflowers are petals, but sepals may also be showy.

Petals help protect the stamens and pistils, but their main function is to attract pollinators. A pollinator is an animal, usually an insect, that picks up pollen and carries it to a stigma. Petals aid pollination by catching the eye of potential pollinators, by providing landing platforms for flying visitors and by discouraging visits from insects that can't pollinate the flower. Many flowers also attract pollinators by giving off a strong smell and by producing pools of a sugary liquid called nectar. You'll be amazed at the great variety of colours and forms among common wildflowers, and at the intricate ways that pollinators and flowers depend on one another.

Floral Tricksters

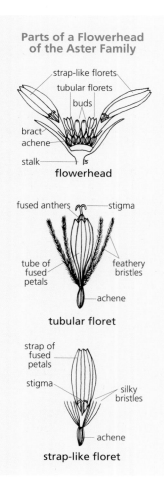

Parts of a Flowerhead of the Aster Family

strap-like florets
tubular florets
buds
bract
achene
stalk
flowerhead

fused anthers — stigma
tube of fused petals
feathery bristles
— achene
tubular floret

strap of fused petals
stigma
silky bristles
— achene
strap-like floret

If a plant has very tiny flowers, one way to attract a pollinator's attention is to produce large, eye-catching clusters. In some cases, these clusters have become so highly developed that they look just like single, large flowers, when they are really compact bouquets of tiny blooms. Flower clusters like these can be confusing when you first try to understand wildflower structure.

In this book, many of the wildflowers that use this trick to get attention belong to the aster family. These plants produce showy *flowerheads* made up of several to hundreds of tiny, stalkless flowers called *florets*. In some cases the petals of each floret are fused into a ribbon-like strap, but florets with tubes of fused petals are equally common.

Flowerheads can be made up entirely of strap-like florets (e.g., common dandelion, p. 70) or of tubular florets (e.g., Canada thistle, p. 61). Typically, however, a flowerhead in the aster family has a central yellow 'button' of tubular florets surrounded by a showy ring of strap-like florets (e.g., oxeye daisy, p. 77). In such two-parted flowerheads, the strap-like florets are commonly mistaken for petals and the central tubular florets are mistaken for stamens. A cross-section of an aster flowerhead is shown at left, along with typical tubular and strap-like florets. A magnifying glass will help you see these structures in a real flowerhead.

Asters aren't the only tricksters among our common wildflowers. Bunchberry (p. 59) and water calla (p. 58) have crowded their tiny flowers into clusters or spikes and surrounded them with showy white bracts that are often mistaken for petals.

Some floral tricksters. *Top left to right:* common dandelion (strap-like florets), Canada thistle (tubular florets), oxeye daisy (strap-like and tubular florets). *Below:* bunchberry and water calla (showy bracts).

Tips for Identifying Wildflowers

1. ***Stop and take a closer look.*** Each wildflower has its own distinctive character, but it's easy to miss important features if you can't see the details. Examine the flower or flower cluster. How big is it? How many petals does it have? Looking closely at a plant will help you with tips 2, 3, 4 and 5.

2. ***Decide which flower group your plant belongs to (pp. 18–19).*** Then, page through the corresponding section of the book until you find a plant like yours. You may need to understand the flower's structure to do this, so be sure to look closely and watch out for tricksters (see p. 12 and above).

3. ***Check the colour guide to the flowers (pp. 4–9).*** This handy section shows small photos of all 112 wildflowers arranged by colour for quick comparison. Flower colour can vary, so be sure to check the written description for possible variations if the picture doesn't seem quite right.

4. ***Try the illustrated wildflower key (pp. 26–35).*** Using a key is easy, once you get used to it. It is often a more precise way to identify a plant than a photo. If the key doesn't lead you to your plant, it will at least narrow your choices.

5. ***Check other books.*** This guide includes 112 common wildflowers, but hundreds of others also grow in Manitoba. Many of these other species are close relatives of plants in this guide and look very similar. Even if this guide does not have the exact flower that you are trying to identify, it should give you an idea of the plant group (genus or family) to which it belongs. A list of reference books may be found on p. 153.

6. ***Don't hesitate to ask.*** Local naturalists and gardeners are often happy to help you identify wildflowers, and they can often tell you stories about these fascinating plants.

To Pick or Not to Pick?

Wildflower lovers are often faced with an important question: To pick or not to pick? It is wonderful to take home a bouquet of fresh flowers and it's fun to press flowers for crafts or collections, but it would be wrong to strip our meadows and waysides of their beautiful blooms, leaving none for others to enjoy.

Most wildflowers that grow in open fields and on barren ground are hardy plants, capable of surviving and even thriving under extremely difficult conditions. Some, however, are surprisingly sensitive. For example, when you pick a wood lily, you take the leaves, stalk and all, and the plant dies. Introduced wildflowers tend to be weedier and less sensitive to cutting than native species. Often, introduced plants have adapted to a wide range of habitats and have very few natural enemies in their new home. The diseases and insects that preyed on them in Europe or Asia have usually been left behind. As a result, introduced weeds often spread rapidly, severely damaging crops and natural vegetation. These flowers can, and often should, be picked.

Some common wildflowers are considered harmful to people or property and have been classified as noxious or nuisance weeds. These plants are regulated by the Manitoba Weed Act, the Canada Weed Control Act and the Canada Seeds Act. The legislation requires many such weeds to be destroyed if they grow close to land that is used for agriculture or horticulture or if they somehow interfere with such uses. The table on the next page lists the wildflowers in this guide that are considered noxious or nuisance weeds.

Weedy species—especially those introduced from Eurasia—can usually be collected with little concern about quantities, and noxious weeds can be gathered freely if they are not poisonous or otherwise dangerous. On the other hand, many native wildflowers grow in sensitive habitats or are easily killed by picking. These species should not be picked at all. Still other plants should be gathered only in moderation; for example, take just one flower in every 20.

annual hawk's-beard

This guide helps you decide whether you should pick a wildflower by providing a picking category for each plant (see p. 23).

If you pick an introduced wildflower, and especially one listed in the table on this page, avoid spreading its seeds. It's also best not to plant weedy introduced species in your garden, in case they spread to natural areas.

Always treat native plants with respect, and take only as much as you need. If you just want to press the flowers, take only the flowers and leave the rest of the plant to grow.

Noxious and Nuisance Weeds in This Guide

COMMON NAME	SCIENTIFIC NAME	PAGE NUMBER
spreading dogbane	*Apocynum androsaemifolium*	142
lesser burdock	*Arctium minus*	60
showy milkweed	*Asclepias speciosa*	140
common milkweed	*Asclepias syriaca*	141
hedge false-bindweed	*Calystegia sepium*	147
nodding plumeless-thistle	*Carduus nutans*	62
field mouse-ear-chickweed	*Cerastium arvense*	121
spotted water-hemlock	*Cicuta maculata*	94
Canada thistle	*Cirsium arvense*	61
field bindweed	*Convolvulus arvensis*	146
annual hawk's-beard	*Crepis tectorum*	66
common viper's-bugloss	*Echium vulgare*	143
wormseed wallflower	*Erysimum cheiranthoides*	105
leafy spurge	*Euphorbia esula*	91
brittle-stem hemp-nettle	*Galeopsis tetrahit*	42
curly-cup gumweed	*Grindelia squarrosa*	76
prickly lettuce	*Lactuca serriola*	65
oxeye daisy	*Leucanthemum vulgare*	77
butter-and-eggs	*Linaria vulgaris*	38
purple loosestrife	*Lythrum salicaria*	135
late yellow locoweed	*Oxytropis campestris*	51
showy locoweed	*Oxytropis splendens*	52
meadow buttercup	*Ranunculus acris*	116
dock	*Rumex* spp.	103
bladder campion	*Silene vulgaris*	122
wild mustard	*Sinapis arvensis*	107
tumbleweed mustard	*Sisymbrium altissimum*	106
perennial sow-thistle	*Sonchus arvensis*	69
common tansy	*Tanacetum vulgare*	85
common dandelion	*Taraxacum officinale*	70
western poison-ivy	*Toxicodendron rydbergii*	17
common goat's-beard	*Tragopogon dubius*	71
scentless chamomile	*Tripleurospermum perforata*	78
stinging nettle	*Urtica dioica*	16
white death-camas	*Zigadenus elegans*	112

Danger, Beware!

A beautiful patch of wildflowers may demand a closer look, but before you rush over to investigate, take time to look around for possible dangers. Ditches often harbour broken glass and sharp sticks. Sudden drops may lie hidden under dense plant growth. Cacti and other spiny plants are easily overlooked until discovered by unprotected toes. When soil is bare, slopes can be unstable (especially when they're wet) and may start to slide from under you.

If you are looking at flowers near a road, remember to watch for passing vehicles. It's also unwise to use roadside plants for food or medicine. Plants growing along roads are usually exposed to many different pollutants. Vehicle exhaust and dust settle on plants; runoff from the road carries salt, oil and other pollutants to nearby soil; and pest-control programs can coat plants with herbicides and insecticides. All in all, it's safer and more enjoyable to study plants well away from heavy traffic.

Even in pristine areas, proceed with caution if you are using any plant for food or medicine. Poisonous plants can be confused with edible species. The carrot family (pp. 92–96) is especially dangerous. Some of our most poisonous plants (e.g., spotted water-hemlock, p. 94 and shown in photo, opposite) are very similar to edible plants (e.g., wild parsnip, p. 95). Carelessly consuming plants in the carrot family is a sort of herbal Russian roulette. Never eat any part of a plant unless you are 100% sure of its identity.

Even with good identification, there can be problems. One person may be allergic to a berry that someone else eats all the time. People with special health considerations such as pregnancy or heart problems may be harmed by a plant that others can use safely.

Potentially harmful wildflowers are identified as such in this book. However, two other plants that may harm people do not have showy flowers; their inconspicuousness, in fact, makes them more dangerous. Both can make your skin burn and itch. Learn to recognize these plants:

stinging nettle

Stinging nettle *(Urtica dioica)*. With its inconspicuous clusters of tiny, green to purplish flowers, stinging nettle blends in easily with other plants. It can usually be found in low meadows, ditches, gullies and other places where soils are rich and moist. The four-sided stems reach 1–3 m in height, much taller than most of the mint species with which this plant could be confused. Stinging nettle can be recognized by its opposite, slender-stalked leaves, which have coarsely toothed, lance-shaped to heart-shaped blades 4–15 cm long, and of course by its tiny stinging hairs if you are unfortunate enough to touch the plant. Each hollow hair has a swollen base that contains formic acid, the same chemical that gives attacking ants their sting.

When the hair pierces you, it injects the acid into your skin, causing itching or burning that lasts anywhere from a few minutes to a couple of days. Usually the effect lasts for less than an hour, but it can be very irritating. Don't panic. It should soon go away. Some say that rubbing the sting with the roots of the offending plant will help to reduce the burning, but this cure may be more psychological than physical.

Western poison-ivy *(Toxicodendron rydbergii)*. Western poison-ivy is a low, bushy herb 10–40 cm tall, with a woody base. It prefers sunny, well-drained sites in ravines, on river flats and in open woods. The plants often form colonies by sending out creeping underground stems. In autumn, the leaves may turn bright red, and white, berry-like fruits may be seen. Poison-ivy is usually recognized by its long-stalked, three-parted leaves. The three pointed leaflets are 3–15 cm long and have smooth or slightly toothed edges. If you're not sure whether a plant is poison-ivy, just remember the rhyme 'Leaves of three, let it be.'

Western poison-ivy will deposit an irritating resin on anything it contacts. The resin can be removed by washing with strong soap and water, but if it is left on skin more than 5–10 minutes, it usually causes a rash. Pets, tools, clothing and even the smoke from burning poison-ivy plants can carry this allergen to unsuspecting victims. Once the rash appears, ointments and antihistamines can help reduce the itching and swelling. Traditional treatments included applying dried blood or the sap from touch-me-not or stinging nettle. Sensitivity varies from one person to the next, and bad cases may require a visit to the doctor.

spotted water-hemlock

western poison-ivy

Organization of the Guide

This guide includes 112 wildflowers common along Manitoba waysides, in pastures and in waste areas such as abandoned lots. Almost all are conspicuous even to highway travellers. A few less noticeable species (e.g., Virginia strawberry) are also included because they are so common.

Two features usually help us recognize flowers: colour and structure. All the wildflowers in this book are organized by colour in the colour guide to the flowers on pp. 4–9, but remember that flower colour can vary. For example, Canada violet (p. 44) may be pink at one site and white at another. Check the flower descriptions for the full range of colours.

Within the book, the wildflowers are divided into five major sections based on the structure of flowers or flower clusters:

Section 1: Two-Sided Flowers (pp. 36–54)

This section includes some of our most unusual flowers. These two-sided, or *bilaterally symmetrical*, flowers can be divided into two equal halves along only a single line. A good example of a two-sided flower is a violet.

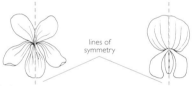

lines of symmetry

violet, pp. 43, 44   bird's-foot-trefoil, p. 49

lady's-slipper, p. 36

Section 2: Tiny Stalkless Flowers in Compact Heads (pp. 55–87)

Some plants have tiny (1–5 mm wide), apparently stalkless flowers in dense, head-like clusters. These clusters, which often appear as individual flowers, are called *flowerheads*. A daisy, for example, is a flowerhead, not a single flower. (See 'Floral Tricksters,' p. 12.)

Most wildflowers in Section 2 belong to the large and variable aster family. These plants have flowerheads ranging from single, huge sunflowers to the scores of small flowerheads in goldenrods. The structure of a typical aster flowerhead is illustrated on p. 12.

There is some overlap between sections 1 and 2, because some members of the pea family (such as clovers, pp. 55–56) have tiny, two-sided flowers that form dense spikes and heads. These flowers are at the beginning of Section 2.

florets

flower-head

sunflower, p. 72   dandelion, p. 70   smartweed, p. 57   bunchberry, p. 59

Section 3: Tiny Stalked Flowers in Branched Clusters (pp. 88–105)

Many flowers are so tiny, you may need a magnifying glass to see them clearly. Even the tiniest blooms, however, become conspicuous if there are enough of them. The individual flowers in this section are only 1–5 mm wide, but dozens or even hundreds of them combine to form showy, lacy clusters.

water-parsnip
p. 93

meadow-rue
p. 102

bedstraw
p. 100

dock
p. 103

Section 4: Circular Flowers with Distinct Petals (pp. 106–141)

When most people think of a flower, they think of a plant from this section. Circular, or *radially symmetrical*, flowers can be divided into two equal parts along two or more lines. The circular flowers in Section 4 are more than 5 mm across and have corollas that are divided at least halfway to their bases, so their petals stand out clearly as individual parts. Section 4 includes a great variety of flowers, ranging from pond-lilies to milkweeds.

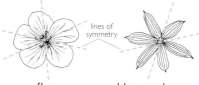

lines of symmetry

flax
p. 134

blue-eyed-grass
p. 110

milkweed
pp. 140, 141

pond-lily
p. 114

Section 5: Circular Flowers with Fused Petals (pp. 142–147)

This relatively small section includes funnel-shaped and bell-shaped flowers. These circular (radially symmetrical) flowers are more than 5 mm across and have corollas that are fused for more than half their length, creating a tube-like structure often tipped with the petal lobes.

harebell
p. 145

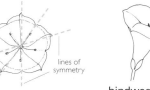

lines of symmetry

bindweed
pp. 146, 147

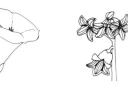

dogbane
p. 142

Information for Each Species

The following information is provided for each wildflower in this guide.

COMMON AND SCIENTIFIC NAMES

Each entry begins with a common name for the wildflower. This name is widely used and generally accepted in our region for that particular plant.

Most plants, and especially most widespread plants like the ones in this guide, have lots of common names. Many wildflowers have long histories, so it's not unusual for a species to have 20 or more common names. Different names can evolve in different regions, at different times and in reference to different uses or stories. You may already know some of these plants by other names.

The common name is followed by the scientific (Latin) name for the species. Although scientific names may be hard to pronounce and remember at first, they are much less confusing than common names in the long run. Generally, a species has only one accepted scientific name, and this name can be changed only when research shows that the original classification was wrong or that an earlier name was overlooked. Scientific names are much less changeable than common names because they have to be presented in reputable publications and accepted by taxonomists (scientists who study classification) before they can be established. Publication also helps keep track of all scientific names that have ever been used for a plant, so it's possible to trace the origins of these names and avoid confusion. Best of all, scientific names apply all over the world, so people who speak different languages can all use the same name.

The family name is also given for each species, in the coloured header bar at the top of the page. As the word suggests, a family is a group of related plants. Knowing which family a wildflower belongs to can help you recognize its relatives. For example, once you learn the general features of peas, you can go straight to the pea family (pp. 45–56) when you see a plant with those features. Common family names also have Latin counterparts: the table on p. 154

blue giant-hyssop

lists the common and scientific family names along with page ranges for quick reference.

NOTES

Below the names, each species entry presents some notes of interest about the wildflower. This section will vary greatly, but it includes the following types of information.

Natural History

Wildflowers depend on many different parts of their environment to survive and reproduce. Information about natural history could include interactions between plants and animals. For example, which animals use these plants for food or shelter? How do plants protect themselves from being eaten?

Many common flowers are successful colonizers, so some notes describe how they reproduce. Why has this wild-flower succeeded where others have failed? How are its flowers pollinated to produce seed? How are its seeds carried to new sites? Can it spread in other ways? Many wildflowers have been spread around the world by human activities such as gardening, farming and shipping. Information about immigration tells when the plant arrived, where it spread and how, and whether it has become a troublesome weed.

annual sunflower

Human Uses

Wildflowers have been used by humans for centuries. A wide range of uses may be presented for a species, but it should be stressed that the reliability of the information varies greatly. Much of it comes from very old sources, and few of the uses have been studied by modern-day researchers.

Food and medicine. Many wildflowers have been important to people as food and medicine. The notes may describe where, when and how plants were collected, what parts were used and how they were processed. For example, were the plants eaten raw, pickled, steamed, boiled or fried? Were their healing properties extracted in teas, syrups or tinctures (alcohol extracts), or were plants simply applied in poultices or inhaled as smoke? Perhaps some plants required special preparation, such as removal of tough or spiny outer layers or soaking in lye to neutralize bitter chemicals.

Leaves, stems and buds may be added to salads, sandwiches, stews, soups, stir-fries, cakes, puddings, omelettes, cheeses and teas. Some have been used to thicken gravy or flavour liqueurs. Roots are occasionally eaten raw in salads, but usually they have been cooked as a vegetable or dried and ground into meal. Some roots have been used to make wine, tea or coffee and to flavour other dishes. Edible flowers and flower pollen are usually used simply as a garnish, but starchy, oil-rich seeds have been used widely for food. Many types of seeds can be gathered and ground into meal or flour for making gruel, cakes and breads. Still others can be roasted to make coffee-like drinks.

The wildflowers in this guide have been used to treat a wide array of ailments, from cuts, bruises and burns to dysentery, cancer and multiple sclerosis. Some have been used cosmetically to remove warts and pimples, and many have been used to treat everyday problems such as upset stomachs, headaches, cramps and colds. Over the years, many wild plants have been applied in poultices and lotions to relieve the aches of arthritis and rheumatism. Still others have been used in medicines for heart disease and diabetes. Remember that very few of these wide-ranging medicinal uses have been tested scientifically.

Wild plants should be used as food or medicine only with extreme caution. See the 'Danger, Beware' section on pp. 16–17 and the individual species entries for more information.

common fireweed

Household uses. The range of uses for common plants seems to have been limited only by the imagination of industrious homemakers. Some of the wildflowers in this guide have been used for making soap, deodorant or insect repellent. Others have provided dyes, toys, cosmetics or stuffing for mattresses and pillows. Many have been used as a source of fibre for thread, cord, twine, cloth, rope and even fishnets. The notes may describe where, when and how plants were collected, what parts were used and how they were processed.

Farming. Some plants were brought to North America as sources of animal feed or green manure. The notes for these plants may include livestock preferences, nectar production (for honey) and the importance of plants in soil improvement programs.

Landscaping. Many successful wayside wildflowers are cultivated as hardy ornamentals. Still others are planted on exposed ground to stabilize slopes and enrich soil. The notes about these plants may include advantages or disadvantages of introducing a particular wildflower into your garden, and the importance of some species for landscaping parks and roadsides.

Superstitions and Folklore

Many myths, legends and superstitions have become associated with wild plants. Plant lore is especially well known for Eurasian species because stories have been written down for hundreds of years in that part of the world. Some wildflowers have been used as charms against snakes, witches and other perceived threats. Still others were chewed and rubbed onto bodies as a source of strength, energy and protection from evil forces.

Meaning of Names

Most scientific names are based on Greek or Latin words. These strange-sounding words often tell us something about the history or appearance of the plant. By understanding the name, you can learn something about the wildflower and you may find the name easier to remember. If a name has changed recently, its previous name may be included at the end of the notes.

IDENTIFICATION POINTS

The bottom part of each species entry gives a short description of the plant, focusing on features that are important for identifying it: the colour, shape and size of the plant and its leaves, flowers and fruits. Most of the information in this section is presented in everyday language, but sometimes more technical terms have to be used. If you don't understand a word, look in the illustrated glossary (pp. 148–152) for an easy-to-understand explanation.

Size ranges are given for most of the identifying features. A ruler is printed on the back cover for quick reference.

Blooming times are also given, to let you know when you can expect to see each flower.

HABITAT AND DISTRIBUTION

For each wildflower, you will also find information about where to look for it. This information comes in two parts. The first, 'Habitat,' describes the type of ecosystem where the wildflower usually grows. Most of the plants in this guide thrive on disturbed ground such as roadsides, but many also grow in more natural habitats such as meadows, woods, streambanks and lakeshores. 'Habitat' is followed by 'Distribution,' which describes the geographical range. If the wildflower grows here naturally, this section begins with the word 'native.' If the species has been intro-

yellow marsh-marigold

duced from elsewhere in the world, its distribution begins with the region where it originated, followed by the parts of North America (north of Mexico) in which it now grows wild.

PICKING GUIDELINE

At the very end of the species description, you will find a general guide to how many blooms it is acceptable to pick:

Pick none: for sensitive native wildflowers or those that grow in sensitive habitats. Don't pick these at all, and avoid trampling them.

Pick a few: for common native plants. Take a few blooms, but be sure to leave many more behind for others to enjoy.

Pick freely: for abundant, weedy plants (mainly introduced), some of which are noxious or nuisance weeds. Take all you want!

Some of the plants in this guide may be dangerous to pick because they are poisonous or have spines, hairs, sap or pollen that can irritate skin. These species have the word **caution** in the 'Pick' part of the description. For example, the picking guideline for Canada thistle is 'freely; caution' because this plant is a noxious weed but is covered in sharp spines—take all you want, but look out for the prickles. Yellow marsh-marigold, on the other hand, is sensitive to picking and its sap can irritate sensitive skin. Its picking code is 'none; caution'—you shouldn't pick it, but you wouldn't want to, anyway.

Of course, these categories apply to plants that are well established in the wild. In some regions, wildflowers are planted along highways to add beauty to barren landscapes and to stabilize and improve soils. If an area has been seeded recently, its young plants should be left alone to multiply.

Fun with Flowers

Wildflowers add beauty to fields and waysides, and they add interest to trips and outings. When kids are travelling, it's fun to keep track of all of the different wildflowers along the way. See who can find the first orange, red or purple wildflower, or who can spot the most species in 10 kilometres, 10 minutes or all day.

As you get to know wildflowers, you may want to keep track of which ones you've seen. All of the species in this guide are listed alphabetically by common name in a checklist on p. 155.

It's hard to identify flowers when you're zooming along at highway speed, and it's dangerous to stop on busy roads. Take time for short walks at roadside pullouts and parks: you'll be surprised at what you discover. Better yet, follow the road less travelled. Back roads let you enjoy a relaxed pace and pull over more easily.

Closer to home, get to know the wildflowers in your neighbourhood and watch them as they grow. You may enjoy keeping a nature diary with notes, sketches and pressed leaves and flowers, describing how plants change through the summer and from year to year. Plants are very cooperative: they stay in the same place throughout their lifetime, and they stand still while you examine them, making them excellent subjects for drawings, paintings and photos.

Everyone enjoys bouquets of freshly cut flowers, and some wildflowers will last for days if they're treated properly. Flowers need to be put into water as soon as possible so they don't wilt. When you pick a plant, it continues to try to draw water up its stem, and air is sucked into the little tubes that transport liquid to the flower. Just before you put your bouquet into water, cut off the bottom few centimetres of each stem to trim off the airlock and allow water to move up the stem to nourish the flowers and leaves. Try adding food colouring to the water, and watch white blooms magically change colour.

With luck, fresh flowers can last for a week, but dried flowers remain beautiful for months or even years. Some flowers preserve better than others. For example, black-eyed Susan and tansy flowers dry well, but more delicate blooms such as golden corydalis and wild blue flax soon fade. Fruit clusters such as the shiny brown capsules of bladder campion and the 'fairy candelabras' of old crane's-bill pods can also add interest to winter bouquets and wreaths.

Many common wildflowers can be dried by simply hanging them in bundles in a warm, dark, dry place. Generally, the more quickly a flower dries, the better its colour will be. If the bundles become too hot, their flowers can scorch and fade, but if they are too cool or damp they may turn brown or mould.

Another way to dry wildflowers is to press them between sheets of absorbent paper such as newsprint. Simply lay the flower between two sheets of paper on a flat surface, put another flat surface over the paper and set a weight on top. Often people press plants in books, but this doesn't always work well; very little air gets to the plant, so the flower and leaves may mould, and the book can be damaged. For better results, make your own plant press. Simply use pieces of corrugated cardboard for your flat surfaces and alternate layers of cardboard, paper, plants, paper, cardboard and so on. When you've laid all your flowers in place, strap or tie the layers together in a snug bundle and set it in a warm place to dry. Air will pass through the tunnels in the cardboard, drying the flowers quickly so that they

keep their colour. If the flowers are bulky, you may need to put a weight on top to help flatten them. If you can't get everything to lie the way you want it to, try pressing the flower for a few hours, then carefully rearrange the petals and leaves while they are still damp.

Pressed flowers are easy to store, and they can be used in many ways. A wildflower collection is a wonderful memento of a trip. Each flower can remind you of a special stop along the way. It's a good idea to write the name of each plant and the place and date you collected it on the pressing paper.

Many craft projects can make use of pressed flowers. The flowers can be glued to paper and covered with clear plastic to make beautiful notecards and bookmarks. Pressed flowers can also be arranged on cardstock and framed behind glass. Similarly, dried wildflowers set between two sheets of glass make lovely wall hangings, sun-catchers and decorations. Pressed clusters of water-parsnip flowers look like delicate snowflakes, perfect for making winter holiday decorations.

The possibilities are endless—just use your imagination!

Using a Key to Identify Wildflowers

A quick and easy way to identify wildflowers is to use a key. Keys ask you questions about the flower you are trying to identify, and you provide the answers. Each answer leads you either to another question or to the name of the wildflower. By using a key, you can narrow your possibilities without having to look through the entire book.

This is a dichotomous key, which simply means that the choices are in pairs so you always choose between two alternatives. For example, read **1a** and **1b**. If the flowers are tiny (1–5 mm across), **1a** is right, so you go to choice **2: 2a** or **2b**. If the flowers are larger, **1b** is correct, so you go to choice **11: 11a** or **11b**. Eventually, you should come to an illustration of your flower. Turn to the page number indicated for that flower to learn more about it.

You can sometimes reach the same answer in more than one way. For example, you may look at a daisy and think that it is a single flower, but someone else may know that it is really a flowerhead made up of many tiny flowers. Some of these potential problems have been taken into consideration in this key, so that you can identify the daisy either way.

If you don't understand some of the words used in the keys or elsewhere in the guide, check the illustrated glossary (p. 148).

Key to the Wildflowers in This Book

Note: In this key, 'petals' refers to all petal-like structures, including true petals, petal-like sepals, petal-like bracts and petal-like florets.

1a Flowers or flower-like heads tiny, usually 1–5 mm across . . . . go to **2a/2b**

1b Flowers or flower-like heads larger (over 5 mm across), single or in showy clusters . . . . go to **11a/11b**

2a Flowers in head-like clusters or spikes; individual flowers stalkless or stalks too short to be seen . . . . go to **3a/3b**

2b Flowers in looser clusters that are branched and often lacy; individual flowers or small (1–5 mm) flowerheads clearly stalked . . . . . . go to **9a/9b**

3a Flower clusters appearing to be individual flowers, made up of a dense central clump of tiny flowers surrounded by a ring of showier, petal-like flowers or bracts . . . . go to **4a/4b**

3b Flower clusters head-like, made up of tiny flowers that are all similar . . . . go to **6a/6b**

4a Flowerheads large and showy, usually at least 2 cm across . . . go to **5a/5b**
4b Flowerheads smaller, 0.5–2 cm across, but forming showy branched clusters

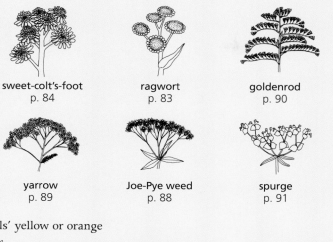

sweet-colt's-foot
p. 84

ragwort
p. 83

goldenrod
p. 90

yarrow
p. 89

Joe-Pye weed
p. 88

spurge
p. 91

5a 'Petals' yellow or orange

sunflower
p. 72

black-eyed Susan
p. 73

blanketflower
p. 74

gumweed
p. 76

false-golden-aster
p. 75

5b 'Petals' white, pink or blue

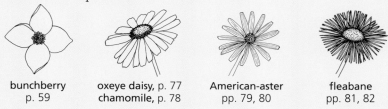

bunchberry
p. 59

oxeye daisy, p. 77
chamomile, p. 78

American-aster
pp. 79, 80

fleabane
pp. 81, 82

6a Each tiny flower not flat and petal-like, usually pea-like or with a tube of
fused petals, but sometimes too tiny to tell . . . . go to **7a/7b**
6b Each tiny flower appearing to be a single flat petal, its true petals fused
into a ribbon-like strap

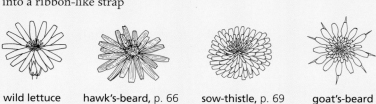

wild lettuce
pp. 64, 65

hawk's-beard, p. 66
hawkweed, pp. 67, 68

sow-thistle, p. 69
dandelion, p. 70

goat's-beard
p. 71

7a 'Petals' expanded and showy . . . . go to **8a/8b**
7b Petals inconspicuous, often hidden by bristles or absent altogether

burdock	pineappleweed	tansy	pussytoes	calla
p. 60	p. 86	p. 85	p. 87	p. 58

8a Each tiny flower with a slender tube of fused petals

burdock	thistle	plumeless-thistle	blazingstar	Joe-Pye weed
p. 60	p. 61	p. 62	p. 63	p. 88

8b Each tiny flower funnel-shaped and/or 2-lipped (not tubular), often with enlarged, spreading 'petals'

giant-hyssop	sweet-clover	alfalfa	clover	smartweed
p. 101	p. 53	p. 54	pp. 55, 56	p. 57

9a Flower clusters wide, with flat or rounded tops, often umbrella-shaped
. . . . go to **10a/10b**
9b Flower clusters somewhat elongated, usually tapered to a point at the tip

goldenrod	wallflower	meadow-rue
p. 90	p. 105	p. 102

bedstraw	false-toadflax	dock	pepper-grass
p. 100	p. 98	p. 103	p. 104

10a Flower clusters with many main stalks radiating from one point (like ribs on an umbrella), each stalk tipped with a similar, smaller cluster of stalks (members of the carrot family)

cow-parsnip, p. 92
parsnip, p. 95

water-parsnip
p. 93

water-hemlock
p. 94

heart-leaved
Alexanders, p. 96

10b Flower clusters differently branched

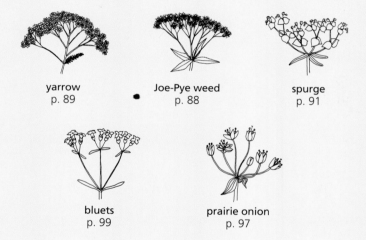

yarrow
p. 89

Joe-Pye weed
p. 88

spurge
p. 91

bluets
p. 99

prairie onion
p. 97

11a Flowers or flower-like clusters 2-sided (bilaterally symmetrical), divisible into 2 equal parts along a single line through the centre, usually with an upper and a lower lip . . . . go to **12a/12b**
11b Flowers or flower-like clusters round or star-shaped (radially symmetrical), divisible into 2 equal parts along 2 or more lines through the centre
. . . . go to **15a/15b**

12a Flowers or flower clusters with sac-like and/or fused petals or a single large bract . . . . go to **13a/13b**
12b Flowers violet- or pea-like, with 5 separate petals including 1–2 upper petals, 2 side (wing) petals and a lower lip formed by 1–2 petals
. . . . go to **14a/14b**

13a Flowers somewhat funnel-shaped, with all petals fused for at least half their length into a cone or tube

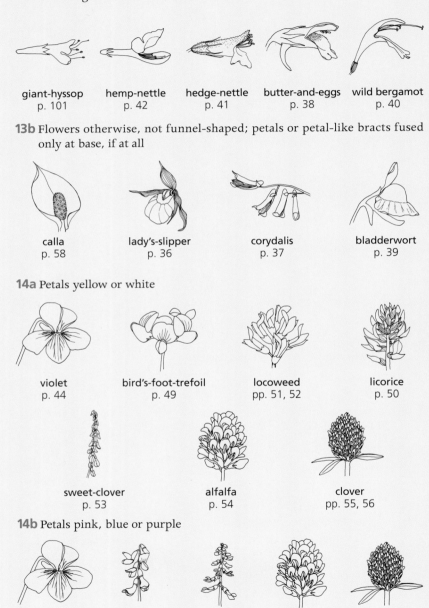

| giant-hyssop | hemp-nettle | hedge-nettle | butter-and-eggs | wild bergamot |
| p. 101 | p. 42 | p. 41 | p. 38 | p. 40 |

13b Flowers otherwise, not funnel-shaped; petals or petal-like bracts fused only at base, if at all

| calla | lady's-slipper | corydalis | bladderwort |
| p. 58 | p. 36 | p. 37 | p. 39 |

14a Petals yellow or white

| violet | bird's-foot-trefoil | locoweed | licorice |
| p. 44 | p. 49 | pp. 51, 52 | p. 50 |

| sweet-clover | alfalfa | clover |
| p. 53 | p. 54 | pp. 55, 56 |

14b Petals pink, blue or purple

| violet | vetchling | sweet-vetch, p. 45 | alfalfa | clover |
| pp. 43, 44 | pp. 47, 48 | vetch, p. 46 | p. 54 | pp. 55, 56 |

15a 'Petals' separate for at least half their length, appearing as distinct petals
· go to **16a/16b**

15b Petals fused for more than half their length to form funnels or bells

dogbane
p. 142

viper's-bugloss
p. 143

bluets
p. 99

bluebells
p. 144

harebell
p. 145

bindweed
pp. 146, 147

16a Flowers (really flowerheads) with 10 or more 'petals' · · · go to **17a/17b**
16b Flowers or flowerheads with 0–9 'petals' · · · · · · · · · · · go to **20a/20b**

17a Flowerheads with a ring of 'petals' (actually tiny flowers) surrounding
a distinctly different centre of many compact tubular florets
· go to **18a/18b**
17b Flowerheads composed of one type of petal or tiny flower
· go to **19a/19b**

18a 'Petals' yellow or orange

sunflower
p. 72

black-eyed
Susan, p. 73

blanket-
flower, p. 74

gumweed
p. 76

false-golden-
aster, p. 75

ragwort
p. 83

18b 'Petals' white, pink or blue

oxeye daisy, p. 77
chamomile, p. 78

American-aster
pp. 79, 80

fleabane
pp. 81, 82

sweet-colt's-foot
p. 84

19a 'Petals' flattened, strap-like

hawk's-beard, p. 66
hawkweed, pp. 67, 68

wild lettuce
pp. 64, 65

sow-thistle, p. 69
dandelion, p. 70

goat's-beard
p. 71

19b 'Petals' tubular or 2-lipped

plumeless-thistle
p. 62

thistle
p. 61

burdock
p. 60

pussytoes
p. 87

blazingstar
p. 63

alfalfa
p. 54

clover
pp. 55, 56

20a Flowers with 3 or more showy 'petals' . . . . go to **21a/21b**
20b Flowers or flowerheads with 0–2 showy 'petals'

burdock
p. 60

pineappleweed
p. 86

tansy
p. 85

spurge
p. 91

21a Flowers with 3 or 6 'petals' . . . . go to **22a/22b**
21b Flowers with 4, 5 or a varying number of up to 9 petals
. . . . go to **23a/23b**

22a Flowers small, 0.6–3 cm across

| arrowhead
p. 109 | blue-eyed-grass
p. 110 | false-Solomon's-
seal, p. 111 | death-camas
p. 112 | purple loosestrife
p. 135 |

22b Flowers large, usually more than 4 cm across

| wood lily
p. 113 | pond-lily
p. 114 |

23a Flowers with 5 'petals' or varying from 5 to 9 'petals' . . . go to **24a/24b**
23b Flowers cross-shaped, always with 4 'petals'

| mustard
p. 107 | tumbleweed mustard
p. 106 | bunchberry
p. 59 |

| fireweed
p. 136 | butterflyweed
p. 138 | evening-primrose
p. 137 | beeplant
p. 120 |

24a Flowers and leaves alternately attached (1 per stem joint)
. . . . .go to **25a/25b**
24b Flowers and leaves paired or whorled (2 or more per stem joint)

campion
p. 122

mouse-ear-chickweed
p. 121

yellow-loosestrife
p. 124

milkweed
pp. 140, 141

25a 'Petals' not yellow . . . . go to **26a/26b**
25b 'Petals' yellow

marsh-marigold
p. 115

buttercup
p. 116

yellow avens
p. 126

silverweed, p. 127
plains cinquefoil, p. 128

shrubby cinquefoil
p. 130

26a 'Petals' white

anemone
p. 117

strawberry
p. 132

white cinquefoil
p. 129

grass-of-Parnassus
p. 119

buck-bean
p. 108

Labrador-tea
p. 139

26b 'Petals' orange, pink, blue or purple

globe-mallow
p. 123

crane's-bill
p. 133

rose
p. 131

three-flowered avens
p. 125

flax
p. 134

prairie-crocus
p. 118

Yellow Lady's-Slipper

Cypripedium parviflorum

This beautiful orchid is widespread but never common, so it is always an exciting discovery. You may be tempted to transplant lady's-slippers to your garden, but please leave them for others to enjoy. Orchid roots grow with special fungi (mycorrhizae) that help them take nutrients from the soil. If the orchid's specific fungus doesn't grow in your garden, neither can the orchid. • The unusual flowers are designed to trap insects. Bees and flies enter easily through the mouth of the slipper, but once inside they slide down smooth, steep walls. Eventually, they discover a hairy strip and follow it

out, but along the way they must first hit the stigma (female part) and then pick up a sticky clump of pollen from the male part. • This species has also been called *C. calceolus.*

Plant: erect perennial 20–80 cm tall, from fibrous roots Leaves: oval to lance-shaped, 6–20 cm long, with sheathing bases Flowers: with 4 (3 separate, 2 fused) purplish brown to greenish yellow, 3–8 cm tepals around a yellow, 2–5 cm, pouched lip; 1–2 flowers per stalk Blooms: May to July Fruits: oblong capsules containing some 15,000 seeds Habitat: moist roadsides and woodlands Distribution: native across North America and around the world Pick: none

Golden Corydalis

Corydalis aurea

This low-growing, early-blooming wildflower flourishes on newly broken ground, but it soon disappears as other plants move in. • Golden corydalis was sometimes used as medicine. Some tribes inhaled the smoke from smouldering roots to clear congestion. Others used the sprawling, grey-green plants to make teas for illnesses ranging from sore throats, stomachaches and headaches to bronchitis, dysentery and heart disease. Many of the alkaloids in golden corydalis are similar to those in the opium poppy, so they have been intensively studied. Unfortunately, some of these compounds are also poisonous. No one has died from eating golden corydalis, but large quantities can cause trembling, staggering and convulsions. • Gardeners have soaked watermelon seeds in golden corydalis tea to increase production. • This plant is sometimes called scrambled-eggs.

Plant: much-branched annual or biennial, with sprawling to ascending stems 20–50 cm long, from a slender taproot
Leaves: mostly twice pinnately divided into 3-lobed leaflets 1–3 cm long **Flowers:** golden yellow, 1–1.6 cm long, tubular with a 4–5 mm pouch (spur) at the base; flowers in compact clusters 1–3 cm long **Blooms:** May to July **Fruits:** slender, cylindrical pods 1.5–2.5 cm long, narrowed between shiny black, 2 mm seeds **Habitat:** open, often rocky sites
Distribution: native from Quebec to Alaska to West Virginia and Texas **Pick:** a few

Butter-and-Eggs

Linaria vulgaris

Butter-and-eggs is a native of Asia and became popular in Europe as a hardy ornamental plant that added a lot of colour and needed little care. It has been very successful on our continent, where it spreads rapidly by seed (up to 8700 per plant) and by creeping underground stems. • Its acrid juice makes butter-and-eggs distasteful to animals and potentially poisonous to humans. In Scandinavia, the plants were boiled in milk to make an insecticide used for attracting and poisoning flies. • Only large insects, such as honeybees and hawk moths, are strong enough to open the lips of these flowers and have tongues long enough to reach the nectar. If you hold a flower up to the light, you can see the nectar in its spur. • This plant is sometimes called toadflax, a name that in Old English translated as 'useless flax.'

Plant: erect, greyish green perennial 30–80 cm tall, from creeping roots **Leaves:** many, alternate (lower leaves sometimes paired), slender, tapered to a stalk-like base, 2–6 cm long **Flowers:** snapdragon-like, 2–3.5 cm long, yellow with an orange lower lip and a slender, yellow, backward-pointing tube (spur); many flowers in compact spikes **Blooms:** May to September
Fruits: rounded, 8–12 mm capsules containing winged seeds **Habitat:** dry, disturbed ground **Distribution:** Eurasia; naturalized from Newfoundland to Alaska to Texas **Pick:** freely

Greater Bladderwort

Utricularia macrorhiza

You may be pleasantly surprised to discover clusters of small, yellow, snapdragon-like flowers on ponds and in ditches. These flowers may seem unusual, but the most exciting part of the plant lies hidden underwater. Bladderworts are carnivorous plants, and their leaves form some of the most sophisticated traps in the plant kingdom. In greater bladderwort, some leaflets form elastic-walled bladders no more than 5 mm across. When a tiny aquatic animal, such as a protozoan, swims by, trigger hairs cause a flaplike door to spring open, sucking the unsuspecting passerby into the bladder. The flap closes and the plant quickly digests its prey. Within an hour or two, the animal is gone and the trap is reset. • The bladders gave rise to the genus name, from the Latin *utriculus*, 'small bottle.' *U. macrorhiza* has also been called *U. vulgaris* var. *americana*.

Plant: floating aquatic perennial with branched stems 30–80 cm long
Leaves: underwater, 2–5 cm long, repeatedly pinnately divided into slender segments, many with bladders 3–5 mm long
Flowers: yellow with brown stripes on the upper lip, snapdragon-like, 1.5–2.5 cm long; in clusters of 6–15, held well above the water on stout stems **Blooms:** June to August **Fruits:** small capsules on arching stalks **Habitat:** calm water
Distribution: native from Newfoundland to Alaska south through the U.S. **Pick:** none

Wild Bergamot

Monarda fistulosa

European settlers and Native peoples gathered this aromatic plant for flavouring salads, cooked vegetables and stews and for making a pleasant minty tea. Dried, powdered leaves were sprinkled on food to keep flies and other insects away and were rubbed onto hair, skin, clothing and even favourite horses as perfume. The plant's fragrance was likened to that of bergamot (the citrus used to flavour Earl Grey tea), giving rise to the name wild bergamot. Settlers soon began planting this beautiful, useful herb and introduced it to England in 1744 as an edible ornamental and tea flavouring. Since then, many hybrids have been developed, providing a variety of long-lasting, rose pink to deep red blooms for bouquets of cut flowers. • Wild bergamot will attract butterflies and humming-birds to the garden. It is best grown from seed.

Plant: grey-green, square-stemmed perennial 50–120 cm tall, from spreading rootstock **Leaves:** paired, lance-shaped, toothed, stalked, 6–10 cm long, smaller upwards **Flowers:** lavender to purple or yellowish pink, 2–3.5 cm long, tubular, with a 3-lobed lower lip and a slender, fuzzy, 2-lobed upper lip tipped with 2 projecting stamens; flowers in head-like clusters **Blooms:** June to September **Fruits:** 4 small nutlets **Habitat:** upland wooded and open sites **Distribution:** native from Quebec to B.C. to the southern U.S. **Pick:** a few

Hairy Hedge-Nettle

Stachys pilosa

This showy, hardy perennial makes an attractive addition to wildflower gardens, but beware! The spreading rootstock can quickly carry the plant to places it isn't wanted. • Although hairy hedge-nettle is rather fuzzy, unpleasant-smelling and bitter-flavoured, all parts of the plant are reputed to be edible. Young plants are the most tender, and boiling helps to reduce the smell, so usually young shoots were cooked. Plump, crisp root-stocks were collected in autumn and eaten raw, boiled, baked or pickled. Traditionally, hairy hedge-nettle was used in poultices, oint-ments and syrups to stop bleeding, heal wounds and relieve cramps, joint pain and dizziness. However, its main qualification as a healing herb was its disagreeable, 'medici-nal' smell. • This species is some-times included in *S. palustris*, which is called marsh hedge-nettle.

Plant: soft-hairy, often glandular perennial 30–100 cm tall, with 4-sided stems
Leaves: paired, 3.5–9 cm long, blunt-toothed, mostly stalkless **Flowers:** pale rose to purplish or whitish, with red blotches, 1.1–1.6 cm long, funnel-shaped, with a hooded upper lip and a flared, 3-lobed lower lip; borne in circles (whorls) of 2–6 in loose spikes 5–15 cm long
Blooms: June to August **Fruits:** 4 nutlets
Habitat: wet sites **Distribution:** native from Quebec to Alaska to the southern U.S. and around the world **Pick:** a few

Brittle-Stem Hemp-Nettle

Galeopsis tetrahit

This prickly immigrant was common in Canada by 1884. Today, it is classified as a weed in Alberta, Manitoba, Quebec and Alaska. • In European kitchens, the stems, roots and flowers were used to make tea and to season meat, and the leaves provided a spring potherb. In merry old England, distilled water from hemp-nettle flowers was said to make the heart merry, the face rosy and the vital spirits fresh and lively. Similarly, plants boiled in wine were applied as hot plasters to remove hardness from the spleen (the seat of melancholy). Modern-day herbalists usually suggest brittle-stem hemp-nettle as a remedy for coughs and congestion, a tonic for blood disorders, a sedative for hyperactive children, an appetite stimulant and a breath freshener. For relief from severe hiccups, try chewing a few hemp-nettle leaves.

Plant: bristly-hairy annual 30–80 cm tall; stems coarse, with swollen joints
Leaves: paired, ovate to lance-shaped, 3–12 cm long, coarse-toothed, stalked
Flowers: pink, white or variegated, often with 2 yellow spots, tubular, 1.5–2.2 cm long, with a rounded upper lip and 3-lobed lower lip; flowers whorled in upper leaf axils, often forming spikes **Blooms:** July to August **Fruits:** 4 nutlets in an enlarged 5–11 mm long calyx with 5 spine-tipped lobes **Habitat:** open, disturbed sites
Distribution: Eurasia; naturalized from Newfoundland to B.C. to the northern U.S.
Pick: freely

Early Blue Violet

Viola adunca

Early blue violet's delicate blossoms hold one of the loveliest wildflower fragrances. Enjoy it while you can. The flower's perfume doesn't fade, but your sense of smell is soon dulled by a substance called ionine. In a few moments the perfume returns, only to disappear again just as quickly. • The leaves and flowers of all violets are edible, but many wild species are too small for gathering. Violet flowers make beautiful garnishes in salads or punch bowls. They can also be candied or used to make purplish jelly and vinegar. • Violet leaves contain more vitamin A than spinach, and one-half cup of violet leaves offers as much vitamin C as four oranges.

Plant: low perennial 2–8 cm tall when flowering
Leaves: basal and on flowering stalks, heart-shaped, usually 1–2.5 cm wide, blunt-toothed; stalks with 2 slender, toothed lobes (stipules)
Flowers: purple to blue with a white throat, 2-lipped, with 5 separate petals and a 4–6 mm backward-pointing spur, side-petals hairy, 8–15 mm long; flowers single on slender stalks **Blooms:** May to July **Fruits:** 4–5 mm long capsules, shooting out brown seeds **Habitat:** moist to dry, sandy or gravelly sites **Distribution:** native from Labrador to Alaska, south through the western U.S. **Pick:** a few

Canada Violet

Viola canadensis

Some tribes tell of a mythical hero who fell in love and stole a girl from her tribe. As the couple fled, the girl wound her braids around her neck to show that she and her lover were married, and her enraged tribe killed them both on the spot. The following spring a new flower, the violet, appeared with the girl's hair etched on its petals. The violet became a symbol of love, courage and devotion, known as 'heads entangled.' • Fine lines on violet petals guide insects to nectar in the spur via a path that ensures pollination. If no pollinators arrive, the violet produces tiny, scentless flowers later in the summer. These never open but rather pollinate themselves, thus ensuring a seed crop. • Each seed has an oily part that ants find irresistible. The ants carry seeds to their nests, eat the oily bits and discard the rest, thereby planting new violets. • *V. canadensis* has also been called *V. rugulosa*.

Plant: perennial 10–40 cm tall, from ascending to creeping rootstock **Leaves:** heart-shaped, 2–10 cm long, coarsely toothed, mostly long-stalked **Flowers:** white to pale pink, with purplish veins and a yellow throat, 1.5–2.5 cm across, 2-lipped, with 5 separate petals and a 4–6 mm backward-pointing spur; side-petals hairy; flowers single in upper leaf axils **Blooms:** April to July **Fruits:** egg-shaped capsules **Habitat:** moist woods and meadows **Distribution:** native from Newfoundland to Alaska to Georgia and Arizona **Pick:** a few

American Sweet-Vetch

Hedysarum alpinum

The 'sweet' in sweet-vetch could refer to the beautiful, fragrant flowers of these plants or to the sweet, edible roots. American sweet-vetch roots are best from autumn to spring, when they contain stored sugars and other nutrients for the plant. As the growing season progresses, these food reserves support the rapidly growing plant, and the roots become tough and dry. When the plant shuts down for winter, it moves nutrients back to the roots for winter storage, and they soon grow crisp and sweet again. • These nutritious, carrot-flavoured roots were a popular food and trade item among Native peoples and were eaten raw, boiled, baked or fried. American sweet-vetch roots are also a favourite food of bears, lemmings and mice. Mice sometimes store large quantities, and people learned that an easy way to gather roots in winter was to train their dogs to sniff out mouse caches hidden under the snow. • This plant has also been called alpine sweet-vetch and *H. americanum*.

Plant: perennial, with erect or ascending stems 15–80 cm long, from taproot **Leaves:** with prominent veins on the lower side, pinnately divided into 11–21 leaflets; leaflets 1–3 cm long **Flowers:** reddish purple to pinkish, pea-like, 1–1.8 cm long; hanging in elongated clusters **Blooms:** June to August **Fruits:** flattened, winged pods, narrowed and jointed between seeds, usually 4–6-seeded **Habitat:** open, well-drained sites **Distribution:** native from Newfoundland to Alaska to the northern U.S.; also in Asia **Pick:** a few

American Vetch

Vicia americana

The name *Vicia* comes from the Latin *vincio*, 'to bind together,' referring to the twining tendrils of these plants. • Sometimes American vetch is confused with veiny vetchling (p. 47) because both plants have reddish purple, pea-like flowers, and both climb over other plants using tendrils. The easiest way to tell a vetch from a vetchling is to look at the tiny style between the two lower petals. In vetches, the style tip has a bottle-brush cluster of hairs, whereas in vetchlings the hairs are all on one side, so the style looks like a tiny toothbrush. • Tender young American vetch plants were sometimes baked or boiled as greens, but this common wildflower was not widely used. Some tribes steeped the roots to make a love medicine; others blew smoke from burning plants into the nostrils of horses to increase the animals' endurance.

Plant: climbing perennial 20–80 cm tall, often in tangled masses **Leaves:** pinnately divided into 8–14 leaflets plus 2 toothed, semitriangular stipules at the base and a well-developed, forked tendril at the tip; leaflets strongly veined, 1.5–3.5 cm long, pointed **Flowers:** reddish purple (drying blue), pea-like, 1.5–2.5 cm long, with a pointed keel much shorter than the side-petals; 2–9 flowers in loose, elongating clusters **Blooms:** June to July **Fruits:** flat, hairless pods 2–4 cm long, with dark, round seeds **Habitat:** open to semishaded sites, often in woods **Distribution:** native from Quebec to Alaska to Texas **Pick:** a few

Veiny Vetchling

Lathyrus venosus

Early settlers in Canada's northern bush soon discovered that this showy vine was a valuable source of fodder for livestock. The seeds were reportedly eaten like peas in the 1600s. • Some tribes believed that veiny vetchling roots were a charm for success, said to be especially effective if someone was extremely anxious about the outcome of a problem. • Native peoples boiled the dried, powdered roots to make medicinal teas for treating convulsions and bleeding. If only a small amount of tea could be forced into the patient's mouth, the medicine was also rubbed onto the chest, the palms and the soles of the feet. A couple of centimetres of root usually sufficed for making medicines. People also drank a dilute mixture as a stimulating tonic. • Veiny vetchling has also been called wild peavine.

Plant: slender, climbing perennial 50–100 cm tall, with tangled masses of 4-angled stems
Leaves: pinnately divided into 8–12 paired leaflets plus 2 small stipules and tipped with a branched tendril; leaflets elliptic, 2–6 cm long, veiny and finely hairy underneath **Flowers:** purple, pea-like, 1–1.8 cm long; in dense, elongating clusters of 15–20
Blooms: June to July **Fruits:** veiny, pea-like pods 4–5 cm long **Habitat:** moist, semishaded sites
Distribution: native from Quebec to B.C. and from Alaska to Texas **Pick:** a few

Cream-Coloured Vetchling

Lathyrus ochroleucus

Many members of the pea family are poisonous, but there is little information about the toxicity of most wild species. Early settlers considered cream-coloured vetchling a 'locoweed,' and therefore bad for horses, but some Native peoples fed it to their ponies to make them lively for races. Although this vetchling can provide some fodder, it is less palatable than many other plants and its seeds may be poisonous. Some tribes used the roots for food and medicine, but given the questionable toxicity of vetchlings in general, such uses are not recommended. • The roots have nodules containing bacteria that convert nitrogen from the air into a form that plants can use, so cream-coloured vetchling helps to enrich soil.

Plant: sprawling perennial, with slender stems up to 1 m long **Leaves:** tipped with tendrils and pinnately divided into 6–10 oval leaflets 2–5 cm long, plus 2 large, almost heart-shaped lobes (stipules) at the stalk base **Flowers:** yellowish white, pea-like, 1.2–1.8 cm long; hanging in 5–10-flowered clusters from leaf axils **Blooms:** May to July **Fruits:** pea-like pods about 4 cm long **Habitat:** moist, open or wooded sites **Distribution:** native from Quebec to Alaska, south to the northern U.S. **Pick:** a few

Bird's-Foot-Trefoil

Lotus corniculatus

This cheerful roadside wild-flower was brought to North America for fodder and honey. In the Middle Ages, bird's-foot-trefoil was recommended as a potherb, but eventually it fell out of favour, perhaps because the raw leaves and flowers contain cyanide. Nineteenth-century herbalists began recommending the plant as a sedative when a distressed woman tried to use it to treat her inflamed eyes and instead found herself cured of insomnia and heart palpitations. No medicinal uses have been clinically proven. • *Corniculatus*, meaning 'small horn,' may refer to the tiny, pointed seed pods. Many fanciful common names for this weed compare its slender, spreading pods to toes or fingers. 'Trefoil' comes from the Latin *tria foliola*, which means 'three leaflets'—although this particular trefoil has five leaflets.

Plant: erect to sprawling perennial 10–60 cm tall **Leaves:** with 5 ovate, 5–15 mm long leaflets (3 at the tip and 2 near the stalk base) **Flowers:** bright yellow, sometimes tinged red, pea-like, 1–2 cm long; 3–6 flowers in flat-topped clusters on slender, 5–10 cm stalks **Blooms:** June to August **Fruits:** slender pods about 2.5 cm long, palmately arranged **Habitat:** moist, disturbed sites **Distribution:** Eurasia; naturalized across temperate Canada and through the U.S. **Pick:** freely

American Licorice

Glycyrrhiza lepidota

For centuries, the thick, sweet-tasting roots of American licorice have provided food and medicine. The flavour and active ingredients in American licorice are similar to those of Eurasian licorices *(G. glabra, G. uralensis)*, and these plants have been used in many of the same ways. People chewed licorice root as a sweet, thirst-quenching nibble, or they used it to flavour candies, root beer and tobacco. Roasting concentrates the flavour. • For thousands of years, *Glycyrrhiza* species have been among the most popular medicines in China. Licorice has often been used to flavour bad-tasting preparations, and studies have confirmed its effectiveness in treating asthma, bronchitis and stomach ulcers. It was even shown to be as effective as codeine for controlling coughs. However, licorice should always be used in moderation. Large doses raise blood pressure.

Plant: coarse, erect perennial 30–100 cm tall, from taproot and creeping rootstock
Leaves: dotted with glands, pinnately divided into 11–19 leaflets; leaflets lance-shaped, 2–4 cm long, abruptly sharp-pointed **Flowers:** yellowish white, pea-like, 1–1.5 cm long; in dense, erect, 2–6 cm long clusters from leaf axils **Blooms:** May to July
Fruits: reddish brown, bur-like pods 1–2 cm long, covered in dense, hooked bristles
Habitat: open, moist, well-drained sites
Distribution: native from Maine to B.C., south through the U.S. **Pick:** a few

Late Yellow Locoweed

Oxytropis campestris

The name locoweed refers to the reputed ability of these plants to drive animals loco, or crazy. Large amounts of these plants must be eaten over a long period of time to produce fatal results, but some animals become addicted to locoweed and will eat little else. In some regions, late yellow locoweed causes more livestock losses than all other poisonous plants combined. Locoweed toxins vary from one species to the next, but one of the best known is the alkaloid locoine. In addition to their alkaloids, locoweeds may accumulate selenium from the soil, and this element is also poisonous in large amounts. • Late yellow locoweed, also called northern yellow locoweed, is one of the most common and complex locoweeds in Canada. Several earlier species, including *O. cusickii*, *O. jordalii*, *O. macounii*, *O. spicata* and *O. varians*, are now classified as varieties of *O. campestris*.

Plant: tufted perennial 10–40 cm tall
Leaves: basal, 6–23 cm long, with 15–33 narrowly oblong to lance-shaped leaflets covered in flat-lying hairs **Flowers:** pale yellow to yellowish white, occasionally pinkish to bluish, pea-like, 1.2–1.7 cm long; 10–30 flowers in dense clusters 2–4 cm long
Blooms: June to July **Fruits:** hairy pods 1.5–2.5 cm long, thinly stiff-walled when mature **Habitat:** open to sparsely wooded sites **Distribution:** native from Newfoundland to Alaska to Colorado **Pick:** a few

Showy Locoweed

Oxytropis splendens

Locoweeds are easily distinguished from other flowers in the pea family by the sharp point at the tip of the keel—the lowermost pair of petals that lies hidden between the two wing petals. In fact, the name *Oxytropis* comes from the Greek *oxys*, 'sharp,' and *tropis*, 'keel,' referring to this pointed tip. • The Blackfoot called locoweed 'rattleweed' because they used the seeds in ceremonial rattles, and because ripe seed pods rattle when shaken. Rattleweed tea was given to children with asthma, especially if their breathing rattled. • Showy locoweed is one of our prettiest and most distinctive locoweeds. It is easily identified by its purplish flowers and silver-haired, whorled leaflets. This beautiful, showy plant thrives in dry, exposed sites, so it makes an excellent addition to rock gardens and dry prairie gardens. Germination improves greatly when the tough seed coat is scratched (e.g., with sandpaper) before planting.

Plant: tufted, silky-hairy perennial 7–35 cm tall, from deep taproot **Leaves:** basal, 7–26 cm long, with oblong-elliptic to lance-shaped leaflets in 7–15 pairs or groups, at least a few in whorls of 3–6 **Flowers:** reddish purple to blue, pea-like, 1–1.5 cm long; 12–35 flowers in dense clusters 3–10 cm long **Blooms:** July **Fruits:** woolly, egg-shaped pods 8–17 mm long
Habitat: open, well-drained sites
Distribution: native from Ontario to Alaska to New Mexico **Pick:** a few

Sweet-Clover
Melilotus officinalis

Sweet-clover is a hardy, drought-resistant forage crop, known for its ability to improve poor soils. It is also highly valued as a honey plant, hence the name *Melilotus*, from the Greek *meli*, 'honey.' Its abundant, fragrant blossoms produce large amounts of nectar. Once pollinated, a plant can produce as many as 350,000 seeds, some even capable of surviving for more than 80 years.
• Sweet-clover leaves and flowers emit a vanilla-like scent and have been used to enhance desserts and drinks, especially teas. The leaves also flavour Gruyère cheese, snuff and tobacco. Only dried plants should be used for these purposes. Mouldy sweet-clover contains the toxic anticlotting agent dicoumarin, which was used to develop the rodent poison warfarin. • White-flowered sweet-clover has been called *M. alba*.

Plant: slender, taprooted biennial (sometimes annual) 50–200 cm tall, with branched stems **Leaves:** with 3 oblong to lance-shaped, blunt-tipped, 1–2.5 cm leaflets that are sharply toothed on the upper half **Flowers:** yellow or white, narrowly pea-like, 4.5–7 mm long; in many narrow clusters 3–8 cm long **Blooms:** May to September **Fruits:** egg-shaped pods about 3 mm long, usually 2-seeded **Habitat:** open, disturbed ground **Distribution:** Europe; naturalized across North America **Pick:** freely

Alfalfa

Medicago sativa

Alfalfa is a valuable fodder and green-manure plant that originally came from western Asia. It was planted in Greece as early as 490 BC; Spanish conquistadors later introduced it to Mexico and Chile. Nowadays, alfalfa is perhaps best known for its tender, delicately flavoured sprouts, which are popular in salads and sandwiches. The mature plants are rich in protein, trace minerals, vitamins (A, C, D, E and K), folate and fibre. They have been used to make a nutritious but rather tasteless tea for treating many ailments, from water retention to cancer, though none of these medicinal uses has been clinically proven. • Alfalfa should be consumed in moderation because it contains substances that may affect liver function and sensitivity of the skin to sun. • 'Alfalfa' is a Spanish word originally derived from the Arabic *al-fasfasah*, 'best fodder.'

Plant: deep-rooted perennial up to 1 m tall
Leaves: with three 1.5–3 cm leaflets (each tipped with teeth) and 2 slender, toothed lobes (stipules) at base of stalk
Flowers: violet blue (var. *sativa*) or yellow (var. *falcata*), 6–12 mm long, on 2–3 mm stalks, narrowly pea-like, with 5 petals and 5 slender sepals; flowers in dense, round to cylindrical, stalked clusters **Blooms:** June to September **Fruits:** small pods, tightly coiled in 1.5–4 turns (var. *sativa*) or hooked or straight (var. *falcata*) **Habitat:** disturbed ground **Distribution:** Eurasia; naturalized across North America **Pick:** freely

Alsike Clover

Trifolium hybridum

Carpets of alsike clover stabilize the poor soils along many roads. This plant also improves the soil because clover roots have small nodules with specialized nitrogen-fixing bacteria (see p. 48). • Alsike clover is widely planted for fodder, food and medicine. The whole plant is rich in protein but difficult to digest, especially in large quantities; boiling helps. The tender white flower bases make a sweet nibble, and the dried flowerheads are used to make tea or are ground into flour. Research suggests that blood thinners found in clover may be useful for treating heart disease. • Each so-called 'flower' is actually a compact cluster of many tiny tubular flowers. These flowerheads bloom from the bottom up, and once pollinated, the flowers droop down, forming a skirt around the base of the cluster.

Plant: perennial 30–80 cm tall **Leaves:** with 3 blunt-tipped, elliptic leaflets and 2 conspicuous, slender-tipped lobes (stipules) at base of stalk; upper leaves with shorter stalks **Flowers:** pinkish to white (brown with age), 7–10 mm long, distinctly stalked, narrowly pea-like, with 5 petals and 5 slender sepals; flowers in head-like clusters on 2–8 cm stalks **Blooms:** May to August **Fruits:** inconspicuous, 1–6-seeded pods **Habitat:** disturbed ground **Distribution:** Eurasia; naturalized across North America **Pick:** freely

Red Clover

Trifolium pratense

If you're looking for a lucky four-leaved clover, try searching in a patch of red clover. Not only are four-parted leaves more common in this species, they are also extra large. This European native is often planted for forage and for green manure. Its long, tubular flowers depend on long-tongued bumblebees for pollination, so when red clover was introduced to New Zealand and Australia, crops failed until bumblebees were imported too. This species is seldom used for food today, but whole plants, young leaves and flowers are all said to be edible, though difficult to digest. Never consume red clover in the fall, when the plants may look normal but contain toxic compounds.
• Red clover has long been used medicinally, as an ingredient in cough remedies and as a tonic, sedative and anticancer agent.

Plant: short-lived perennial up to 80 cm tall
Leaves: with 3 ovate leaflets (broadest above the middle) and 2 slender-pointed basal stalk lobes (stipules); upper leaves short-stalked **Flowers:** magenta to almost white, 1.3–2 cm long, stalkless, narrowly pea-like, with 5 petals and 5 slender sepals; flowers in stalkless or short-stalked heads 1.3–2.5 cm long **Blooms:** May to August
Fruits: inconspicuous, 1–6-seeded pods
Habitat: disturbed ground
Distribution: Europe; naturalized across North America **Pick:** freely

Water Smartweed

Polygonum amphibium

This widespread aquatic plant grows wild on every continent except Australia. It is an important food for migrating waterfowl, which carry its seeds around the world. • Some tribes used these beautiful pink flower clusters as trout bait, while others dried and smoked them as a hunting charm to attract deer. • The name *Polygonum*, from the Greek *polys*, 'many,' and *gonu*, 'knee,' refers to the knobby stems. Because of its 'many-kneed' appearance, Europeans once believed that smartweed was good for swollen, painful joints. Water smartweed is rich in astringent tannins and in flavonoids that slow bleeding and lower blood pressure. Native peoples used this plant to treat mouth sores, stomachaches, diarrhea and even peyote poisoning. • Water smartweed has also been called swamp persicaria.

Plant: aquatic to terrestrial perennial, with spreading 50–100 cm stems from rootstock **Leaves:** somewhat leathery, floating or spreading, 5–15 cm long; stalks with basal lobes forming a 1–2 cm long cylinder around the stem **Flowers:** bright pink to scarlet, with 5 petal-like sepals; flowers numerous, in 1–3 cm, oblong to egg-shaped spikes **Blooms:** July to August **Fruits:** dark brown, 2.5–3 mm, lens-shaped, seed-like achenes **Habitat:** calm, shallow water and shores **Distribution:** native from Newfoundland to Alaska, south through the U.S. and around the world **Pick:** none

Water Calla

Calla palustris

All parts of this beautiful plant contain tiny, sharp crystals of calcium oxalate. In the mouth and digestive tract, these crystals inflame soft tissues and cause an intense burning sensation. Because of this, animals rarely take more than one mouthful. • Despite the plant's fiery-hot nature, calla berries and rootstocks have been used for food. In Scandinavia, rootstocks were dried, ground, boiled and then mixed with powdered fir inner bark and baked in loaves. The resulting 'missen bread' was said to be as tough as rye bread but sweet and white. • Some tribes believed that people who wetted their hands with the milky root juice of water calla could safely handle rattlesnakes. • *Calla* comes from the Greek *kallos*, 'beautiful.' The ancient name water-dragon seems equally appropriate.

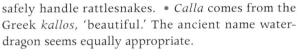

Plant: aquatic perennial, from creeping rootstock **Leaves:** basal, ovate to heart-shaped, 5–10 cm long; stalks 7–20 cm long **Flowers:** tiny, yellowish, lacking petals and sepals; many flowers in a 1.5–2.5 cm long cylinder (spadix) at the base of a showy, white bract (spathe); spathe white, abruptly pointed, 2.5–7 cm long **Blooms:** June to July **Fruits:** red, berry-like, in dense heads 1.5–5 cm long **Habitat:** calm, shallow water **Distribution:** native from Newfoundland to Alaska to the northeastern U.S. and around the world **Pick:** none; caution

Bunchberry
Cornus canadensis

Bunchberry makes a lovely groundcover in shady wildflower gardens. Each cheerful little 'flower' is, in fact, a miniature bouquet of tiny blooms surrounded by four showy bracts that look like petals. The bright white bracts lure pollinators to the true flowers, which are so tiny that they are easily overlooked. The bracts also provide landing platforms for insects carrying pollen from other plants. In late summer, dense clusters of small, red berries replace the flowers. Some people enjoy these juicy fruits, with their crunchy little seeds, but others consider them mealy and tasteless. Bunchberries can be eaten as a trail nibble or added to puddings and sauces.

Plant: colonial perennial 7–20 cm tall, from creeping rootstock **Leaves:** 4–8 cm long, with deep, arched veins; in circles (whorls) of 4–6 at stem tips **Flowers:** tiny, greenish yellow to purplish, clustered at centre of 4 white, petal-like bracts; each flower-like cluster 2–4 cm across **Blooms:** late May to July
Fruits: red, berry-like drupes, 6–8 mm long, in tight clusters **Habitat:** moist, often acidic sites **Distribution:** native from Newfoundland to Alaska to the northern U.S. and in eastern Asia and Greenland **Pick:** a few

Lesser Burdock

Arctium minus

Lesser burdock arrived in New England in 1638, and by the end of the 19th century its sticky seed heads had carried it to western North America. • This burdock and others were used to treat everything from kidney problems and rheumatism to psoriasis and dizziness. The large leaves provided poultices for skin problems, and the seeds were applied to bruises, venomous bites, and sores. • The fleshy taproots of first-year plants can be eaten raw or boiled as a vegetable. Burdock roots have also been dried, roasted until brown and ground as a coffee substitute. Like artichokes, burdock roots contain the complex carbohydrate inulin, which breaks down to fructose. The white stem pith is also edible raw, steamed, roasted, boiled or even simmered in sugar to make candy. *Note:* Pregnant women and diabetics should not use burdock.

Plant: coarse biennial with hollow stems 30–150 cm tall **Leaves:** somewhat woolly underneath, up to 50 cm long, ovate to heart-shaped, stalked **Flowerheads:** bur-like, 1.5–2 cm across, with slender, pink or purplish tubular florets projecting from the tip of a spherical cluster of greenish to purplish, hooked bracts; flowerheads in branched, elongated clusters **Blooms:** July to October **Fruits:** seed-like achenes **Habitat:** disturbed sites **Distribution:** Eurasia; naturalized across the U.S. and southern Canada **Pick:** freely

Canada Thistle

Cirsium arvense

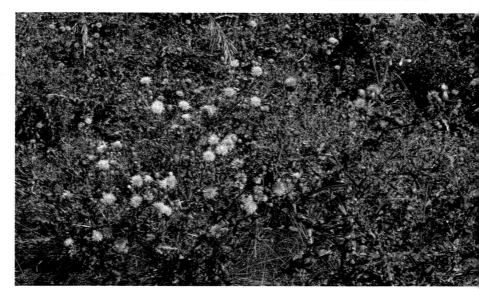

Despite its name, Canada thistle is not a native plant. It arrived here from Eurasia in the 1700s and spread south to the U.S., where it was given its common name. • This is our only thistle with colonies of male or female plants. Deep underground runners shoot out rapidly—up to 6 m per plant per year—sending up as many as 200 shoots in the first summer. New shoots often stand in lines radiating from the parent plant, but soon they grow their own runners, and the area becomes blanketed in a thistle maze. One female plant can produce up to 40,000 seeds, each one capable of surviving 20 years or more. Not only can thistles reproduce rapidly, they have protective spiny leaves that are usually left to flourish, undisturbed by grazing animals.

Plant: prickly perennial 30–150 cm tall
Leaves: sometimes white-woolly underneath, wavy-edged or lobed, spiny-toothed
Flowerheads: rose purple to white, 1.5–2.5 cm across; florets all tubular, above a 1–2 cm cup of overlapping, pointed to spine-tipped bracts; flowerheads in branched clusters
Blooms: June to September **Fruits:** seed-like achenes with white, feathery bristles
Habitat: disturbed sites **Distribution:** Eurasia; naturalized from Newfoundland to Alaska to New Mexico **Pick:** freely; caution

Nodding Plumeless-Thistle
Carduus nutans

This aggressive colonizer arrived in North America early in the 1900s and is now a troublesome weed. Nodding plumeless-thistle spreads rapidly by seed, sometimes forming extensive colonies that reduce crop and rangeland productivity by 100%. • In Europe, dried nodding-thistle flowers are still used to curdle milk in cheese-making, giving rise to another name, milk thistle. When mashed flowers are soaked in water for 5–6 hours and the liquid is added to warm (50° C) milk, the milk curdles in about 30 minutes. • Like true thistles (*Cirsium* spp.), plumeless-thistles taste rather like artichokes. With their spines removed, young stems, leaves and flowerheads can be eaten raw in salads or steamed and served hot.

Plant: erect biennial, with spiny-winged stems 30–200 cm tall **Leaves:** prickly, 7–25 cm long, irregularly sharp-toothed and lobed, with lower edges extending down the stem **Flowerheads:** rose purple, 4–6 cm across; florets all tubular, above overlapping rows of broad (2–8 mm), spine-tipped, down-curved bracts; flowerheads nodding, long-stalked, usually single **Blooms:** June to October **Fruits:** seed-like achenes with white, finely barbed bristles **Habitat:** disturbed sites **Distribution:** Eurasia; naturalized from Newfoundland to B.C., south through the U.S. **Pick:** freely; caution

Dotted Blazingstar

Liatris punctata

This long-lived plant makes a lovely addition to prairie gardens. It is best grown from seed, and mature plants can be trimmed to increase bushiness. • Although the thick, carrot-flavoured roots are edible, most tribes considered them survival food only. Roots were gathered in early spring; after that they became too dry and woody. Dotted blazingstar roots were also used in teas for treating kidney problems, stomachaches and sore throats. Smoke from smouldering roots was inhaled to stop nosebleeds and to relieve headaches. • The epithet *punctata*, from the Latin word *punctum*, 'point,' refers to the tiny, translucent, puncture-like marks (glands) on the leaves. Some tribes called this plant 'crow root' because they believed crows and ravens ate the roots. Another common name is dotted gayfeather.

Plant: clumped, grey-green perennial 10–60 cm tall, with erect to sprawling stems from a thick, corm-like root crown on a stout taproot to 4.5 m deep
Leaves: stiff, slender, 3–15 cm long, densely dotted, fringed with white hairs
Flowerheads: purple to rose, about 1.2–1.5 cm across, with 4–6 tubular florets in a cup of overlapping bracts; numerous flowerheads in dense spikes **Blooms:** late July to September **Fruits:** hairy, grey-black, seed-like achenes 6–7 mm long, tipped with a cluster of feathery bristles **Habitat:** dry, open sites **Distribution:** native from Manitoba to Alberta to Texas **Pick:** a few

Common Blue Lettuce

Lactuca tatarica

The scientific name *Lactuca*, from the Latin *lac*, 'milk,' refers to the milky sap of these plants. This sap was said to heal pimples and other skin problems and to soothe stings. People who have sensitive skin, however, may develop rashes from lettuce sap. Although these plants have been eaten raw in salads or cooked as potherbs, their milky sap soon becomes very bitter, and older plants are quite tough. Some tribes dried sap from the roots, rolled it into balls and chewed it like gum. • Common blue lettuce is sometimes grown from seed in wildflower gardens, but plant with caution. It often becomes weedy, and its deep, creeping rootstocks make it hard to control. • This species has also been named *L. pulchella*. *Lactuca* species are also called horseweeds, because horses are said to favour them.

Plants: erect, blue-green perennial 20–80 cm tall, from rootstock **Leaves:** slender, 5–18 cm long, often with a few backward-pointing lobes, stalkless **Flowerheads:** blue, up to 2.5 cm across, with 18–50 strap-like florets above a 1–2 cm long tube of green bracts; flowerheads in open, branched clusters **Blooms:** July to September **Fruits:** seed-like achenes 4–7 mm long, tipped with a stout beak bearing a parachute of silky white hairs **Habitat:** moist, open, often disturbed sites **Distribution:** native from Nova Scotia to Alaska, south through the U.S. and around the world **Pick:** a few; caution (irritating sap)

Prickly Lettuce

Lactuca serriola

Common garden lettuce *(L. sativa)* was probably developed from prickly lettuce. Young leaves of this plant have been eaten in salads or cooked as a vegetable, but they are usually too bitter for most tastes. The bitter, milky sap (latex) contains rubbery compounds, and prickly lettuce was once considered as a commercial source of rubber, but it proved uneconomical. • Herbalists use the dried sap as a mild sedative and painkiller; it has even been used to treat opium addiction. Many sources recognize the weak narcotic qualities of lettuce sap, but studies supporting its use as a medicine are lacking. In any case, the tedious process of collecting and drying a usable amount of sap would require a great deal of patience. • Prickly lettuce is also known as a 'compass plant'; the vertical upper leaves are said to align north–south.

Plant: bristly-prickly annual or biennial 30–150 cm tall **Leaves:** spiny-toothed, deeply lobed, often twisted to stand vertically on edge; upper leaves smaller and often clasping **Flowerheads:** yellow (drying blue), about 6 mm across, with 14–24 strap-like florets from a tubular, 1–1.5 cm long cluster of green bracts; flowerheads in many-branched clusters **Blooms:** July to September **Fruits:** spiny-ribbed, seed-like achenes with stalk-like beaks supporting silky white parachutes **Habitat:** disturbed sites **Distribution:** Eurasia; naturalized from Quebec to B.C. to Texas **Pick:** freely; caution (irritating sap)

Annual Hawk's-Beard

Crepis tectorum

This widespread weed was introduced to the New World from Siberia. The first Canadian records came from New Brunswick in 1877, and today the yellow flowerheads of this successful invader dot roadsides across North America. One plant can produce more than 49,000 seeds, which can begin growing as soon as they hit the ground. Annual hawk's-beard is considered to be a troublesome weed in Manitoba and Alberta, but it is rarely a problem in cultivated fields. Instead, it usually invades forage crops, pastures and roadsides. • Although the leaves of various hawk's-beards have been eaten (usually cooked), some European species are believed to cause nervous disorders, so these plants are better left alone. • Annual hawk's-beard has also been called narrow-leaved hawk's-beard.

Plant: erect annual 10–50 cm tall, with branched stems from taproot
Leaves: lance-shaped, 10–15 cm long, edged with backward-pointing teeth or pinnate lobes; smaller and simpler upwards
Flowerheads: yellow, 1–1.5 cm across, with 30–70 strap-like florets above a 6–9 mm high cluster of inwardly hairy bracts; 5 to many flowerheads in open, flat-topped clusters **Blooms:** June to July
Fruits: burgundy, seed-like achenes 3–4 mm long, spindle-shaped, 10-ribbed, tipped with a parachute of whitish hairs
Habitat: open, usually disturbed sites
Distribution: Eurasia; naturalized across North America **Pick:** freely

Narrow-Leaved Hawkweed

Hieracium umbellatum

This common wildflower could be confused with annual hawk's-beard (p. 66), but hawk's-beard has smaller (1–1.5 cm wide) flowerheads, paler green flower bracts and white (not tawny) hairs on its fruits. • The cut leaves and broken stems and roots of hawkweeds exude a milky sap (latex) that is rich in rubber. Some tribes chewed dried balls of sap or simply the plants themselves like chewing gum. • Although hawk-weeds' flowerheads attract pollinating insects, they can often seed without fertilization. This type of reproduction (apomixis) can create classification nightmares for scientists by producing thousands of almost identical plants. More than 2400 minor species of *Hieracium* have been described from Britain and Scandinavia. • This species has also been called Canada hawkweed and *H. scabriusculum*.

Plant: erect to ascending perennial 20–100 cm tall, with milky sap and leafy stems **Leaves:** narrowly oblong to ovate, 3–8 cm long, toothed to almost smooth-edged; upper leaves often clasping the stem **Flowerheads:** bright yellow, 2–2.5 cm across; florets all strap-like, above an 8–12 mm high cluster of smoky green to blackish, over-lapping bracts; flowerheads 1 to many in open clusters **Blooms:** July to September **Fruits:** ribbed, seed-like achenes 3 mm long, tipped with a tuft of soft, brownish hairs **Habitat:** open, often disturbed sites **Distribution:** native from Nova Scotia to B.C. to the central U.S. and around the world **Pick:** a few

Orange Hawkweed

Hieracium aurantiacum

In Britain in the 1600s, orange hawkweed was planted as a novelty ornamental for its bright orange flowerheads and its black, hairy stalks.
Although it is not used as a medicine today, at that time orange hawkweed
was boiled in water or wine, which was then drunk or applied externally to
heal wounds. • Today, this common wildflower is often called devil's paint-
brush. Its flowerheads resemble tiny brushes dipped into orange paint, and
it can be a devil of a weed. A very successful colonizer, orange hawkweed
reproduces from seed, from spreading underground stems and from trailing
runners. • The name *Hieracium*, from the Greek *hieros*, 'hawk,' refers to the
ancient myth that hawks ate these plants to improve their vision.

Plant: erect, bristly-hairy, 1- to several-stemmed
perennial 10–60 cm tall, with milky sap
Leaves: basal, tufted, 5–15 cm long
Flowerheads: red-orange, 1.5–2.5 cm across;
florets all strap-like, above a cluster of bracts with
stiff, black, often gland-tipped hairs; flowerheads
in compact, branched clusters of 5–30
Blooms: June to August **Fruits:** ribbed, seed-
like achenes with a tuft of soft, brownish hairs
Habitat: disturbed sites **Distribution:** Europe;
naturalized in southeastern Canada and the
northeastern U.S. **Pick:** freely

Perennial Sow-Thistle

Sonchus arvensis

Some say the young shoots and leaves of this common weed provide one of the best wild salads, but older leaves and flower buds are best boiled for 5–10 minutes. The bright yellow flowerheads provide a colourful garnish. • Perennial sow-thistle spreads rapidly. A single plant can produce 4000 seeds, which mature in only 10 days and can survive for several years. Once they establish, the fleshy, white roots spread horizontally, sending up new shoots. The roots are easily broken, and even small pieces can produce new plants. Additional roots stretch down as deep as 3 m. Sow-thistle competes enthusiastically for nutrients, moisture and light, so even minor infestations can drastically reduce crop yields. • Sow-thistle was so named because pigs apparently like to eat it.

Plant: erect, often blue-green perennial 40–200 cm tall, with milky sap
Leaves: 6–40 cm long, with prickly, deeply lobed edges; smaller, less lobed and clasping upwards on the stem
Flowerheads: yellow, 3–5 cm across; florets all strap-like, above overlapping rows of slender green bracts; flowerheads in widely branched clusters
Blooms: July to October **Fruits:** wrinkled, 10-ribbed, seed-like achenes tipped with silky white parachutes **Habitat:** disturbed sites **Distribution:** Europe; naturalized from Newfoundland to Alaska to Texas
Pick: freely

Common Dandelion

Taraxacum officinale

This successful immigrant has been planted for food and medicine since ancient times in Europe, China and India. The tender young leaves, rich in vitamins and minerals, make good salad or cooked greens. The delicate yellow flowers can be added to fritters and pancakes or made into wine. Dandelion roots provide a raw or cooked vegetable, a caffeine-free coffee substitute and even a red dye. With age, the plants soon grow bitter; leaves in full sun are especially harsh. Pale plants (like those grown in shade or buried in sand) and frost-nipped plants are sweetest. The mildly laxative and diuretic leaves have been used in medicinal teas, digestive aids, diet drinks and rustic beers.

Plant: robust perennial with milky juice, 5–50 cm tall, from taproot **Leaves:** basal, 5–40 cm long, irregularly toothed and lobed **Flowerheads:** yellow, 2–5 cm across; florets all strap-like, above 2 rows of slender, green bracts, the outer row bent backwards; flowerheads single on leafless, hollow stalks **Blooms:** April to September **Fruits:** spiny-ribbed, seed-like achenes with a slender, stalk-like beak bearing a silky white parachute **Habitat:** disturbed sites **Distribution:** Eurasia; a cosmopolitan weed **Pick:** freely

Common Goat's-Beard

Tragopogon dubius

Look for common goat's-beard early and late in the day. Its flowerheads usually open at sunrise and close by midday, but the large, fluffy seed heads are most visible in the evening, when their silky hairs catch the rays of the setting sun. The names goat's-beard and *Tragopogon* (from the Greek *tragos*, 'billy goat,' and *pôgôn*, 'beard') both refer to the fluffy tufts of hair on the seeds. These downy parachutes often carry seeds over great distances on the wind, rapidly spreading the plant to new areas. • Tender young goat's-beard shoots can be eaten raw or cooked, in the same way as asparagus, and the plant bases are sometimes cooked like artichokes. Also, the fleshy roots of first-year plants have been roasted or boiled like parsnips, or chopped raw and added to salads.

Plant: erect biennial 30–100 cm tall, with milky sap **Leaves:** grass-like, tapered from a clasping base to a slender point **Flowerheads:** yellow, 2.5–6.5 cm across; florets all strap-like, above longer, slender-pointed, green bracts; flowerheads borne on swollen stalk tips **Blooms:** May to August **Fruits:** ribbed, seed-like achenes 2.5–3.5 cm long, with a stout beak supporting a parachute of feathery white hairs **Habitat:** open, disturbed sites **Distribution:** Europe; naturalized from Newfoundland to Alaska to Texas **Pick:** freely

Annual Sunflower

Helianthus annuus

Annual sunflower was one of the first plants cultivated in North America. Its oily seeds were usually roasted, shelled and ground into meal for making gruel or bread. Often this meal was mixed with fat and formed into flat cakes. Today, sunflower seeds are popular in breads, cereals, salads and countless other dishes. Although we generally think of only the seeds as edible, the bright yellow strap-like florets make a colourful salad garnish. The leaves and immature flowerheads provide a vegetable with an artichoke-like flavour. In the 1600s, they were reputed to equal artichokes in flavour and surpass them in procuring bodily lust. • The name *Helianthus*, 'sun flower,' refers to the fact that the flowerheads constantly turn to face the sun.

Plant: coarse, rough-hairy annual plant 50–300 cm tall **Leaves:** mostly alternate, ovate to heart-shaped, 6–25 cm long, usually toothed and stalked
Flowerheads: yellow, 5–15 cm across; many strap-like florets surrounding a 3–4 cm, red-brown button of tubular florets, with broad, abruptly slender-pointed bracts at the base; 1 to few flowerheads **Blooms:** July to September
Fruits: 2–4-sided, seed-like achenes 5–10 mm long, containing a white seed
Habitat: moist, disturbed sites
Distribution: native in the western U.S.; naturalized across North America and around the world **Pick:** freely

Black-Eyed Susan

Rudbeckia hirta

Black-eyed Susan is native to the American Midwest, but in the past 100 years it has spread rapidly, probably with hay and livestock, and it is now common from coast to coast. Black-eyed Susan cultivars may be found at most gardening centres. • The cheery orange and brown flowerheads make excellent, long-lasting cut flowers. Be sure, though, to take a pair of scissors along if you want to gather a bouquet because the stems can be quite tough. The blossoms also make wonderful pressed flowers and winter bouquets because they keep their bright orange colour when dried. • The brown tubular florets produce bright yellow pollen. Outer florets mature first, and a thin yellow ring of pollen gradually moves toward the centre of the disc. • This species has also been called *R. serotina*.

Plant: rough-hairy biennial or short-lived perennial 30–100 cm tall **Leaves:** 5–17 cm long, ovate to narrowly oblong, with winged stalks; upper leaves stalkless
Flowerheads: orange-yellow, 5–10 cm across, with 10–20 orange to golden yellow strap-like florets around a dark purple to brown, 1.2–2 cm wide hemisphere or cone of tubular florets; 1 to few flowerheads **Blooms:** June to September
Fruits: seed-like achenes
Habitat: open, often disturbed sites
Distribution: central North America; naturalized from Newfoundland to B.C. to Mexico **Pick:** freely

Great Blanketflower

Gaillardia aristata

As its common name suggests, this vibrant wildflower displays the bold colours of blankets from the American Southwest. Blanketflower can last for days as a cut flower. It is also a beautiful, hardy plant for wild-flower gardens, easily grown from seed or by transplanting leafy (not blooming) plants. Many showy cultivars have been developed. • Blanket-flower plants have been boiled to make medicinal teas for problems ranging from headaches to tuberculosis and cancer. Sometimes, great blanketflower was used to predict a patient's future. When plants were boiled for a long time and the water stayed clear or whitish, the person would die. A red-dish or well-coloured liquid indicated that the patient would recover. • Great blanketflower has also been called great-flowered gaillardia.

Plant: greyish-hairy perennial 20–70 cm tall, from slender taproot **Leaves:** oblong to lance-shaped, 5–15 cm long, smooth-edged to deeply lobed **Flowerheads:** yellow with a purplish centre, 3–7 cm across, with 6–18 broad, yellow (often purple-based), 3-lobed strap-like florets around a domed 1–4 cm button of purplish tubular florets; flowerheads long-stalked, 1 to several **Blooms:** May to September **Fruits:** 3-sided, seed-like achenes, tipped with 5–10 papery scales **Habitat:** dry, open sites **Distribution:** native from Manitoba to B.C. to New Mexico; occasionally naturalized elsewhere **Pick:** a few

Hairy False-Golden-Aster

Heterotheca villosa

This hardy little wildflower thrives in dry, sunny sites, so it does well in prairie gardens without extra watering. Seed is commercially available, or it can be collected from September to October. • Some tribes boiled the fuzzy plants to make a soothing medicinal tea for aiding sleep. The same tea was used as a wash for healing bruises and reducing swelling in the legs. For toothaches, a heated root was applied to ease the pain. • The name *Heterotheca* comes from the Greek *heteros*, 'different,' and *theca*, 'container,' because the seed-like fruits of the outer, strap-like florets are different from those produced by the inner, tubular florets. The species name, *villosa*, means 'shaggy-haired.' • *H. villosa* has also been called *Chrysopsis villosa*, a name taken from the Greek *chrysos*, 'gold,' and *opsis*, 'aspect' or 'face.'

Plant: grey-green, silky-hairy perennial 10–60 cm tall, sometimes glandular, with clumped stems from a woody-crowned taproot **Leaves:** numerous, elliptic to oblong, 2–5 cm long **Flowerheads:** yellow, about 2.5 cm across, with 10–25 strap-like florets around a yellow button of tubular florets, each head with overlapping rows of bracts at the base; 1 to several flowerheads in flat-topped clusters **Blooms:** July to September **Fruits:** hairy, flattened, seed-like achenes tipped with a parachute of silky white hairs **Habitat:** dry, open sites **Distribution:** native from Ontario to B.C., south through the U.S. **Pick:** a few

Curly-Cup Gumweed

Grindelia squarrosa

The fragrance of this plant is most noticeable on hot, sunny days. Like a number of other such resinous plants, gumweed has provided many medicines. The upper stems and leaves were brewed to make teas for coughs, asthma, bronchitis, indigestion and kidney or bladder problems. The resinous flowerheads were pounded or boiled to make poultices or washes for wounds, burns, sores, pimples and poison-ivy rashes. Several patents have been granted for gumweed substances, and the essential oil is in demand for aromatherapy. • Curly-cup gumweed is easily recognized by the gummy, strongly hooked bracts on its flowerheads. The name *squarrosa* means 'rough with outward-projecting tips,' a reference to these bracts.

Plant: aromatic biennial or short-lived perennial 30–60 cm tall, with much-branched stems from taproot **Leaves:** dotted with resin glands, oblong, 1–4 cm long, irregularly toothed or lobed, clasping the stem **Flowerheads:** yellow, 2–3 cm across, with 25–40 strap-like florets around a broad button of tubular florets and with overlapping rows of sticky, backward-curling bracts at the base; numerous flowerheads in flat-topped clusters **Blooms:** July to September **Fruits:** 4–5-ribbed, seed-like achenes, tipped with a few slender bristles (soon shed) **Habitat:** dry, open sites **Distribution:** Newfoundland to B.C., south through the U.S. **Pick:** a few

Oxeye Daisy
Leucanthemum vulgare

This highly successful weed originated in Asia and spread into Europe hundreds of years ago. First introduced to eastern North America in the early 1600s, it is now one of the most common wildflowers across the continent. Many travellers enjoy the cheerful blooms, which fill ditches and blanket fields, but farmers view oxeye daisy as an aggressive weed that rapidly replaces valuable forage plants. • Daisies have long been part of European lore, twisted into daisy chains and circlets at picnics and school commencements, or plucked of their white 'petals' (actually strap-like florets) to the chant 'He loves me, he loves me not.' • This species previously had a lovely rhyming name, *Chrysanthemum leucanthemum*.

Plant: slender, erect perennial 20–90 cm tall, from spreading rootstock **Leaves:** basal and alternate, 4–15 cm long, coarsely toothed or lobed, smaller and stalkless upwards
Flowerheads: white, 2.5–5 cm across; 15–35 strap-like florets around a bright yellow, 1–2 cm button of tubular florets, with dry, brown-edged bracts at the base; flowerheads single
Blooms: May to September **Fruits:** 10-ribbed, seed-like achenes **Habitat:** open, disturbed sites **Distribution:** Eurasia; naturalized from Newfoundland to Alaska to Texas **Pick:** freely

Scentless Chamomile

Tripleurospermum perforata

An aggressive invader of pastures and of hay fields, scentless chamomile is quick to infest cropland. Today, this flourishing immigrant is classified as a noxious weed across western Canada and in Quebec. A single plant can produce more than 300,000 seeds, which may remain dormant for several years, waiting until the time is right to germinate and produce a whole new generation of plants. • At first glance, this species could easily be mistaken for oxeye daisy (p. 77), but upon closer examination, the finely divided leaves will clearly identify scentless chamomile. This plant is also very similar to its well-known but sweetly scented relative, wild chamomile *(Matricaria recutita)*. A tea from this fragrant species has been used for centuries as a pleasant drink and as medicine. • *T. perforata* has also been called *Matricaria perforata* and *M. maritima* (in part).

Plant: erect, nearly scentless annual (usually), biennial or short-lived perennial 10–70 cm tall
Leaves: 2–8 cm long, pinnately divided into slender, often thread-like parts
Flowerheads: white, 2.5–5 cm across; 12–25 strap-like florets around a bright yellow, 8–15 mm hemisphere of tubular florets; several to many flowerheads **Blooms:** July to September **Fruits:** rectangular, 3-ribbed, seed-like achenes **Habitat:** open, disturbed sites **Distribution:** Eurasia; naturalized from Newfoundland to Alaska to the central U.S.
Pick: freely

Fringed American-Aster

Symphyotrichum ciliolatum

This cheerful blue wildflower brightens waysides long after most other blooms have faded. Many different aster-like plants grow wild in Manitoba, but fringed American-aster is one of the easiest to identify. It has distinctive heart-shaped lower leaves with long, fringed stalks. • Native peoples sometimes used this plant for medicine. They boiled the strongly scented roots to make eye drops, and they used the smoke from burning roots to revive people who had fainted in sweat baths. Sometimes a paper cone was used to force the smoke up the nose of an unconscious patient. • The specific epithet, *ciliolatum*, means 'fringed,' a reference to the hairy-edged leaf stalks. *S. ciliolatum* has also been called *Aster ciliolatus*, fringed aster and Lindley's aster.

Plant: erect perennial 20–120 cm tall, from spreading rootstock **Leaves:** 4–12 cm long, pointed; lowest leaves toothed, heart-shaped, with notched bases and slender, hairy-edged stalks; stem leaves lance-shaped, usually stalkless **Flowerheads:** pale blue to purplish, 1.5–3 cm across; 12–25 strap-like florets around a button of yellow tubular florets, with slender bracts at the base; flowerheads in branched, open clusters **Blooms:** July to October **Fruits:** seed-like achenes tipped with a parachute of silky white hairs **Habitat:** woodlands and open, often disturbed sites **Distribution:** native from Quebec to B.C., south to the northern U.S. **Pick:** a few

Smooth Blue American-Aster

Symphyotrichum laeve

Smooth blue American-aster is one of the most common asters in western Canada. In autumn, its showy flowers produce beautiful banks of blue, long after most other wildflowers have faded. This showy plant has great potential as a garden subject, and it is easily grown from rootstock cuttings or from seed (either collected wild or produced commercially). • Some Native peoples used smooth blue American-aster for medicine. Teething babies were given the roots to chew, and people packed rootstock fragments into cavities to relieve toothaches. • 'Aster,' the Greek word for 'star,' refers to the star-shaped flowers. According to ancient legend, asters were created by a god scattering stardust over the landscape. The species name *laeve*, 'smooth,' refers to the hairless plant. *S. laeve* has also been called *Aster laevis* and smooth blue aster.

Plant: erect, hairless, often blue-green perennial 30–120 cm tall, from rootstock **Leaves:** thick, oval to oblong, 2–10 cm long, with winged stalks; upper leaves stalkless, often clasping **Flowerheads:** pale blue to dark purple, 2–3 cm across, with 20 or more strap-like florets around a yellow button of tubular florets and with firm, overlapping bracts at the base; few to many flowerheads in open clusters **Blooms:** July to September **Fruits:** hairless, seed-like achenes tipped with tawny, hair-like bristles **Habitat:** open sites **Distribution:** native from Quebec to the Yukon to Texas **Pick:** a few

Smooth Fleabane

Erigeron glabellus

These showy blue flowerheads make a lovely addition to wild-flower gardens. Smooth fleabane usually produces large quantities of seed with good germination, and it can also be grown by dividing mature plants in spring or fall. • It is often difficult to distinguish flea-banes (*Erigeron* species) from asters (*Aster* species and *Symphyotrichum* species, pp. 79, 80). As a general rule, fleabanes flower earlier than asters, and the strap-like florets of fleabanes are more slender and numerous than those encircling an aster flowerhead. • Fleabane leaves were sometimes used to make salves for relieving pain and swelling. • The name *Erigeron* comes from the Greek *eri*, 'early,' and *geron*, 'old man,' because the flowers appear early in the year and soon produce fluffy grey seed clusters that look like small, grey-haired heads.

Plant: biennial or perennial 10–50 cm tall, from fibrous roots **Leaves:** usually stiff-hairy, widest above the middle, 5–15 cm long; upper leaves smaller and stalkless **Flowerheads:** blue, pink or whitish, 1–2 cm across, with 125–175 slender (up to 1 mm wide) strap-like florets around a button of yellow tubular florets and with slender, hairy bracts at the base; usually 1–3 flowerheads (sometimes up to 10) **Blooms:** June to August **Fruits:** seed-like achenes with a tuft of white to reddish hairs **Habitat:** open sites **Distribution:** native from Ontario to Alaska, south to New Mexico **Pick:** a few

Philadelphia Fleabane

Erigeron philadelphicus

This pretty native wildflower is usually considered a weed to be pulled on sight in gardens and along sidewalks. However, if left to grow, Philadelphia fleabane will produce lovely flowerheads—each ringed with more than 100 slender florets—from late spring to autumn. • In the early 1900s, physicians used oils from the leaves and flower clusters of this plant to speed up contractions and to stop bleeding during births. Philadelphia fleabane has also been used to help control nosebleeds and internal bleeding and to treat fevers, bad coughs, diabetes and even tumours. • The smoke produced by burning some *Erigeron* species was used to drive away fleas and other insect pests, giving rise to the common name fleabane.

Plant: soft-hairy biennial or perennial 15–90 cm tall, from rootstock and runners **Leaves:** blunt-toothed to lobed, 5–15 cm long; lower leaves short-stalked, stem leaves stalkless and clasping **Flowerheads:** rose purple to white, 1–2.5 cm across, with 100–400 slender strap-like florets around a yellow button of tubular florets; flowerheads in branched clusters **Blooms:** April to August **Fruits:** seed-like achenes tipped with a tuft of white hairs
Habitat: various; usually disturbed sites
Distribution: native from Newfoundland to the Yukon to Texas **Pick:** a few

Marsh Ragwort

Senecio congestus

In dry years, vivid yellow skirts of marsh ragwort often ring prairie sloughs and ponds. Usually, these large, hairy plants (also appropriately called woolly-mammoth plant) shoot up to their full height and produce flowers and seeds in a few short weeks. Occasionally frost kills the flowers, and the plants grow again the following year. • Although young plants have occasionally been added to salads or cooked in soups and stews, marsh ragwort should be treated with caution. Some western Inuit believed that the roots were poisonous, and of the nearly 50 species of *Senecio* in North America, 7 are suspected or proven to be toxic. Also, marsh ragwort produces large amounts of highly allergenic pollen; hay fever sufferers beware! • The name *congestus* refers to the compact (congested) flower clusters, and not to this plant's effect on susceptible noses.

Plant: erect annual (occasionally biennial) 20–100 cm tall, with hollow stems from fibrous roots **Leaves:** 5–15 cm long, wavy-edged **Flowerheads:** yellow, 1–2 cm across, with short strap-like florets around a button of tubular florets and with over-lapping, hairy bracts at the base; flower-heads in rounded to flat-topped clusters **Blooms:** June to August **Fruits:** seed-like achenes, tipped with tufted white hairs **Habitat:** open sites near water **Distribution:** native from Newfoundland to Alaska to the north-central U.S., and around the world **Pick:** a few; caution

Arctic Sweet-Colt's-Foot

Petasites frigidus

This feathery white wildflower is one of our first signs of spring. It's hard to believe that such a pretty little plant could cause any trouble, but it has. Sweet-colt's-foot plants are rich in minerals, and their ashes were sometimes used as a salt substitute. In some parts of the southwestern U.S., where salt supplies were limited, control of sweet-colt's-foot colonies sparked rivalries intense enough that battles sometimes ensued. • Sweet-colt's-foot can provide more than just salt. Its leaves and flowering stems, though fuzzy, have been eaten steamed, stir-fried and boiled. The flower clusters can be fried in batter or chopped and tossed into casseroles or soups. *Note:* Pregnant women should not eat this plant or drink sweet-colt's-foot tea. • This widespread, complex species now includes *P. palmatus*, *P. sagittatus*, *P. hyperboreus* and *P. nivalis*. The variety *sagittatus* is shown here.

Plant: erect perennial 10–50 cm tall, from creeping rootstock **Leaves:** basal, 10–30 cm long, arrowhead-shaped and shallowly toothed to smooth-edged, or round to triangular and deeply lobed, white-woolly underneath **Flowerheads:** whitish, about 8 mm across, with few strap-like florets around a cluster of tubular florets; flowerheads in rounded, elongating clusters **Blooms:** May **Fruits:** seed-like achenes with silky hairs, forming fluffy, white heads 2–3.5 cm long **Habitat:** moist to wet sites **Distribution:** native from Labrador to Alaska to Colorado **Pick:** none

Common Tansy

Tanacetum vulgare

Common tansy was one of the first medicinal herbs brought to North America. Traditionally it was used to repel lice and fleas, kill intestinal worms and induce abortions, sometimes with fatal results for mother and child. It has also been used to flavour liqueurs, cakes, puddings, omelettes, salads and cheeses, but now we know it should never be used in food unless its toxins (especially thujone) have been removed. • Common tansy was the herb that made Ganymede, beautiful cup-bearer of the Greek gods, immortal. For that reason, and because of its strong, insect-repelling fragrance, this plant was used to preserve bodies in ancient Greece. • In Canada, common tansy is a troublesome weed. One plant can produce more than 50,000 seeds, and established plants spread rapidly by creeping rootstocks.

Plant: coarse, leafy, aromatic perennial 40–100 cm tall **Leaves:** dotted with glands, 10–20 cm long, pinnately divided into deeply lobed and/or sharply toothed leaflets; short-stalked to stalkless **Flowerheads:** deep yellow, 5–10 mm across; florets all tubular; flowerheads in flat-topped clusters of 20–200 **Blooms:** July to September **Fruits:** 5-ribbed, seed-like achenes **Habitat:** disturbed sites **Distribution:** Eurasia; naturalized across most of North America **Pick:** freely

Pineappleweed
Matricaria discoidea

This aromatic herb is closely related to chamomile *(M. recutita;* see p. 78) and has been used in many of the same ways. Bruised pineappleweed smells like freshly cut pineapple. The fragrant plants make an excellent deodorant, capable of masking even the strong smell of fish when rubbed on hands. Pineappleweed can also be hung as an air freshener, stuffed into pillows and sachets, dropped into hot bath water for an aromatic soak, or rubbed over skin or clothing as perfume and insect repellent. The flower-heads can be nibbled straight from the plant, tossed into salads as a lemony garnish or steeped in water to make a fragrant tea. The tea acts as a mild sedative for inducing sleep and soothing upset stomachs. • *M. discoidea* has also been called *M. matricarioides.*

Plant: leafy, low-branching annual 5–40 cm tall
Leaves: 1–5 cm long, 2–3 times pinnately divided into slender, sometimes thread-like parts **Flowerheads:** yellow, 5–9 mm across, cone-shaped; florets all tubular, above dry, thin-edged bracts; several to many flowerheads
Blooms: May to September **Fruits:** 2-ribbed, often 5-sided, seed-like achenes
Habitat: open, disturbed sites
Distribution: native in the western cordillera; naturalized across most of North America
Pick: freely

Little-Leaved Pussytoes

Antennaria parvifolia

These low-growing plants are either male or female, but male plants are usually rare to non-existent. Fortunately, pussytoes can produce abundant seed without fertilization. Doing so helps the plants spread rapidly, but it also creates a lot of confusion in classification. Three of our most common pussytoes—little-leaved *(A. parvifolia)*, small-leaved *(A. microphylla)* and rosy *(A. rosea)*—are closely related and can be difficult to distinguish.
• Each small flowerhead is tipped with a clump of furry down that looks like the soft, rounded toe of a kitten, hence the name pussytoes. These soft hairs produce little parachutes that carry the tiny, seed-like fruits on the wind. The genus name *Antennaria* comes from the Latin *antenna*, because the club-shaped hairs on male flowers look like insect antennae.

Plant: mat-forming perennial 2–15 cm tall, with leafy creeping stems **Leaves:** densely white- or grey-woolly on both sides, mainly basal, roughly tongue-shaped, 1–3.5 cm long; stem leaves slender, long-pointed **Flowerheads:** whitish; florets all tubular, above a 7–11 mm high cluster of pale, whitish-tipped bracts; flowerheads in compact, rounded clusters **Blooms:** May to July **Fruits:** seed-like achenes, tipped with a tuft of white hairs **Habitat:** dry, open sites **Distribution:** native from Ontario to B.C., south through the western U.S. **Pick:** a few

Spotted Joe-Pye Weed

Eupatorium maculatum

Joe Pye, a 19th-century European, promoted the lifestyle of North American Native peoples and used this plant to cure fevers during a typhus outbreak in New England. Traditionally, the root of Joe-Pye weed was used to increase sweating and urination and to generally cleanse the system, so it was included in treatments for various illnesses, including diabetes, rheumatism and persistent kidney and bladder problems. The dried plants have a vanilla-like fragrance and are said to make a pleasant tea. • Spotted Joe-Pye weed is adapted to capture as much light as possible. Each ring of leaves is staggered so the blades line up with spaces between the leaves below. • *E. maculatum* has also been called *E. purpureum* var. *maculatum*.

Plant: erect perennial 60–200 cm tall, with hollow, purplish stems **Leaves:** in circles (whorls) of 3–5; lance-shaped, 6–20 cm long, coarsely sharp-toothed, short-stalked **Flowerheads:** fuzzy, pinkish purple to pale lavender, about 4–6 mm across, with 9–22 tubular florets above overlapping rows of 3–5-nerved bracts; flowerheads in flat-topped clusters 10–14 cm wide **Blooms:** July to September **Fruits:** seed-like achenes with a tuft of soft hairs **Habitat:** moist, open sites **Distribution:** native from Newfoundland to B.C. to New Mexico; rare in Alberta, Montana and a few southeastern states **Pick:** a few

Common Yarrow

Achillea millefolium

In the Middle Ages, common yarrow was found in every monastery, apothecary shop and household medicine chest, ready to treat anyone who admitted to illness. It was used most often to stimulate sweating, reduce inflammation and stop bleeding.
• The fresh, young leaves also furnished a rather bitter, aromatic salad green. When eaten today, the young leaves are often cooked as a vegetable or potherb, and the older leaves provide a sage-like seasoning or a nourishing tea. Housewives and wild birds alike have used this pungent plant to repel fleas and other insects. Smoke from burning yarrow flowers was said to repel both insects and evil spirits, and smouldering seed heads were used to keep witches at bay.

Plant: aromatic perennial 20–100 cm tall, from spreading rootstock
Leaves: feathery, 3–15 cm long, finely divided, often grey-hairy
Flowerheads: white to pink, 5–6 mm across; 4–6 short strap-like florets around 10–30 yellow tubular florets above overlapping, dark-edged bracts; flowerheads in flat-topped clusters 2–10 cm wide **Blooms:** June to September **Fruits:** hairless, flattened, seed-like achenes **Habitat:** highly variable; often disturbed sites
Distribution: native throughout North America and around the world
Pick: a few

Canada Goldenrod

Solidago canadensis

This eye-catching wildflower has been much maligned as the guilty party in countless hay fever attacks. In fact, goldenrod pollen is too heavy to travel on the wind; insects must carry it. The real hay fever culprits are inconspicuous plants, such as ragweeds (*Ambrosia* species), that flower at the same time. Plants with wind-pollinated flowers often go unnoticed because they don't have showy flowers. • Some large goldenrod colonies are estimated to be about 100 years old. Older, central plants may eventually die back, creating a ring, but usually colonies are too dense for other plants to invade. • Beautiful Canada goldenrod, also known as graceful goldenrod, is rarely grown in Canadian gardens, but it is apparently popular in Europe.

Plant: perennial 25–100 cm tall with finely hairy upper stems, from spreading rootstock
Leaves: 3–15 cm long, 5–20 mm wide, toothed, finely hairy underneath (at least on main veins), stalkless **Flowerheads:** yellow, 2–4 mm across; 10–17 strap-like florets and 2–8 tubular florets above overlapping, green-tipped bracts; flowerheads on 1-sided branches in pyramidal clusters **Blooms:** August to October **Fruits:** seed-like achenes tipped with tufted white hairs **Habitat:** open sites **Distribution:** native from Newfoundland to Alaska to Texas **Pick:** a few

Leafy Spurge
Euphorbia esula

This aggressive weed appeared in Ontario in 1889. A mere 40 years later it had spread to British Columbia, and within a century more than 1 million hectares were infested in North America. With their exploding capsules, leafy spurge plants can shoot seeds up to 5 m away. Seeds also float along streams to establish new colonies. To make matters worse, tiny pieces of the deep, easily broken roots can grow into new plants, and the decaying leaves poison livestock (though sheep seem to be immune). Leafy spurge quickly displaces native plants and reduces rangeland productivity by 50–75%. • The name *Euphorbia* honours Euphorbus, physician to a king of Mauritania in the first century BC. • Take care! The milky juice can burn sensitive skin and may cause blindness if it touches the eyes.

Plant: hairless perennial 30–70 cm tall, from strong, spreading roots **Leaves:** slender, 3–8 cm long, stalkless **Flowers:** tiny, in 2 mm wide groups resembling single flowers; each group has 4 male flowers and 1 stalked female flower in a cup with 4 crescent-shaped glands above 2 petal-like bracts; flower groups in branched, umbrella-shaped clusters with circles (whorls) of leaves at the main base and paired, heart-shaped bracts below smaller sub-clusters **Blooms:** June to August **Fruits:** 3–3.5 mm capsules **Habitat:** disturbed sites **Distribution:** Eurasia; naturalized across temperate North America **Pick:** freely; caution

Common Cow-Parsnip

Heracleum maximum

Although mature cow-parsnip is strong-smelling, many tribes used it for food. Young shoots and stems were peeled, then cooked or eaten raw, often dipped in grease or sugar. Sometimes stalks were roasted in coals and then peeled. The aromatic seeds flavoured soups and stews, and the ashes of burned leaves became a kind of salt. Some people liken the roots to rutabagas, but others find the taste too strong to be enjoyable. • The dried, hollow stems can be used to make elk and moose whistles, children's flutes, drinking straws and toy blowguns, but these items may irritate the lips. People with sensitive skin often develop rashes when contact with cow-parsnip is followed by exposure to bright sunlight. It is a good idea to gather this robust plant with gloves. • *H. maximum* has also been called *H. lanatum*.

Plant: hairy perennial 1–3 m tall, with hollow stems **Leaves:** divided into 3 large (10–30 cm), lobed, toothed leaflets; upper leaf stalks with enlarged bases **Flowers:** small, white; many in twice-divided, umbrella-like clusters 10–20 cm wide, with 15–30 main branches **Blooms:** June to July **Fruits:** flattened, heart-shaped, seed-like schizocarps 8–12 mm long **Habitat:** moist, rich sites **Distribution:** native across North America and in Siberia **Pick:** a few; caution

Common Water-Parsnip

Sium suave

Some tribes believed the smoke from common water-parsnip seeds could drive away evil spirits trying to steal a hunter's luck. The slender, fleshy, nutty-flavoured roots were harvested in early spring and eaten raw or cooked. The leaves are also said to be edible but very strong-tasting. However, water-parsnip is so similar to its highly poisonous relatives (such as spotted water-hemlock, p. 94), it is better left alone. Reports of poisoning most likely come from confusion with toxic species. Water-parsnip has ribbed stems and a circle (whorl) of small bracts at the base of each of its flower clusters; water-hemlock has smooth, rounded stalks and lacks bracts. Unfortunately, by the time a water-parsnip plant is large enough to identify with certainty, its roots are too woody to eat.

Plant: erect perennial 60–200 cm tall, from fibrous roots **Leaves:** pinnately divided into 7–17 narrow, sharply toothed leaflets 5–10 cm long **Flowers:** tiny, white; many in flat-topped, 3–12 cm wide, umbrella-shaped clusters with 6–20 main branches above a ring of 5–8 slender bracts **Blooms:** July to September **Fruits:** oval, corky-ribbed, seed-like schizocarps 2–3 mm long **Habitat:** wet, open sites **Distribution:** native from Newfoundland to Alaska to the southern U.S. and in Siberia **Pick:** none

Spotted Water-Hemlock
Cicuta maculata

One night during his famous western expedition (1857–60), John Palliser heard strange noises coming from a nearby wetland. His Métis companions informed him that the sounds came from the powerful and deadly water-hemlocks that lurked in the swamp. • Spotted water-hemlock is one of our most poisonous wild plants: a single rootstock can kill a horse. Children have been poisoned by using peashooters made from water-hemlock stems. Symptoms include stomach pains, vomiting, weak and rapid pulse and convulsions. If you think someone might have consumed any part of a water-hemlock, take a sample of the plant and seek medical help right away. • Spotted water-hemlock is distinguished by its swollen, chambered rootstocks and yellowish, oily, foul-smelling sap. Also, the main side-veins of the leaves end at the bases of the leaf teeth, and not at the tooth tips. Remember: 'Vein to the cut, pain in the gut!'

Plant: erect perennial 60–200 cm tall, with thick-based stems from fibrous roots
Leaves: 2–3 times pinnately divided into sharply toothed leaflets 3–10 cm long
Flowers: tiny, white; many in 5–12 cm wide, umbrella-shaped clusters, usually without bracts at the base **Blooms:** June to August **Fruits:** round, slightly flattened, corky-ribbed, seed-like schizocarps 2–4 mm long **Habitat:** wet sites **Distribution:** native from Nova Scotia to Alaska to Mexico **Pick:** none (abundant, but very toxic)

Wild Parsnip

Pastinaca sativa

Early settlers brought parsnips to North America as a source of food, fodder and medicine. Although wild parsnip roots are thinner and more aromatic than those of their home-grown relatives, they can still be gathered at the end of the first growing season and used as a sweet, starchy vegetable. Creative Irish cottagers used parsnips to make beer, wine and a marmalade-like preserve. The young shoots are also edible, but older leaves taste too strong. The strong-smelling, oil-rich fruits have been used as a spice. In Britain, parsnips were considered excellent livestock feed, especially good for fattening pigs. • People with sensitive skin can develop rashes if they touch parsnip and then go into bright sunlight.

Plant: erect biennial 60–150 cm tall, with sturdy, grooved stems from a stout taproot
Leaves: pinnately divided into 5–15 large, toothed and lobed leaflets 5–10 cm long
Flowers: tiny, yellow; many borne in 5–20 cm wide, umbrella-shaped clusters with 15–25 main branches; clusters usually lacking bracts at the base **Blooms:** June to September
Fruits: flattened, winged, seed-like schizocarps 5–7 mm long **Habitat:** disturbed ground
Distribution: Eurasia; naturalized across most of North America **Pick:** freely; caution

Heart-Leaved Alexanders

Zizia aptera

Many species that belong to the carrot family (pp. 92–96) have fascinating histories. This widespread wildflower, by contrast, has been largely overlooked by humans. The young flower clusters of some *Zizia* species are reportedly added to salads occasionally, but the most common use for heart-leaved Alexanders has been in the garden. A hardy perennial, it can tolerate alkaline soils and cold winters, but it needs sunshine and consistently moist soil to thrive. Beds where heart-leaved Alexanders is planted should not dry out between waterings. Most gardeners appreciate the attractive, early flowers and the interesting form and texture of the leaves. Seed is commercially available, but it requires a long period of cold treatment to germinate successfully. • The name *Zizia* commemorates Johann Baptist Ziz, a German botanist who lived from 1779 to 1829. *Aptera* means 'wingless,' a reference to the fruits. Heart-leaved Alexanders is also called heart-leaved meadow-parsnip.

Plant: hairless, shiny perennial 20–60 cm tall, from cluster of fleshy roots **Leaves:** mainly basal, heart-shaped, finely toothed, 2–10 cm long, with long stalks; the few stem leaves, once or twice divided in threes, with broad, toothed leaflets **Flowers:** bright yellow, tiny; many in repeatedly divided, umbrella-shaped clusters 2.5–5 cm across **Blooms:** May to July **Fruits:** hairless, narrowly ribbed, seed-like schizocarps 2–4 mm long **Habitat:** moist meadows and prairies **Distribution:** native from Quebec to B.C. to Florida and Nevada **Pick:** a few

Prairie Onion

Allium textile

Although prairie onion is small, it was often so abundant that it was gathered for food by both Native peoples and European travellers. Captain Meriwether Lewis of the Lewis and Clark expedition (1804–06) described the bulbs as crisp, white and about the size of a musket ball. Despite their diminutive size, he was once able to gather half a bushel (about 18 litres) for the camp's supper. • Unlike domestic onions, prairie onion has flat, solid (not hollow) leaves, but it has the same distinctive onion flavour and fragrance as all members of this edible genus. Smell is a good way to avoid confusing wild onions with poisonous relatives such as death-camas (p. 112). If it doesn't smell like an onion, don't eat it. • The species name *textile*, 'woven,' refers to the fibrous coat on the bulbs. Prairie onion has also been called white wild onion.

Plant: pungent-scented, erect perennial 8–25 cm tall, from a small bulb covered in netted fibres **Leaves:** 2, basal, 1–5 mm wide, 10–15 cm long **Flowers:** white (rarely pinkish), lily-like, 5–7 mm long, with 6 tepals; 8–20 flowers in umbrella-shaped clusters **Blooms:** May to July **Fruits:** oblong capsules about 4 mm across, tipped with 6 small knobs **Habitat:** dry, open sites **Distribution:** native from Manitoba to Alberta to New Mexico **Pick:** a few

False-Toadflax
Comandra umbellata

This delicate white flower makes a pretty addition to wildflower gardens. Its innocent appearance, however, belies a sinister side. False-toadflax always grows best near other plants because it locks onto the roots of its neighbours to steal water and nutrients. Many different plants can be hosts for this parasite.
• The fully grown, slightly green fruits are edible, but they are rarely abundant enough to provide more than a nibble. This scarcity is probably for the best, because too many cause nausea, and false-toadflax is known to accumulate toxic levels of selenium when this element is present in soil. Some people find the oily drupes sweet and delicious, while others consider them bland. The ripe, brown fruits are also said to be edible, but less flavourful.
• The leaves and stems have been thought to resemble those of toadflax (butter-and-eggs, p. 38), hence the common names false-toadflax and bastard-toadflax.

Plant: erect, blue-green perennial 10–30 cm tall, in clumps and colonies from creeping rootstock **Leaves:** firm, slender, 1–3 cm long, essentially stalkless **Flowers:** greenish white to pinkish, 3–5 mm across, with 5 pointed petal-like sepals; flowers numerous, in groups of 3–5 in larger, ovoid clusters **Blooms:** May to July **Fruits:** firm, brownish green drupes, 4–8 mm long, tipped with old sepals **Habitat:** gravelly, open slopes **Distribution:** native from Newfoundland to the Yukon to the southern U.S. **Pick:** a few

Long-Leaved Bluets

Houstonia longifolia

When a flower is fertilized by pollen from another plant, it is said to be cross-pollinated. This exchange helps increase genetic variation within a species, thereby producing stronger offspring. Bluets have developed an interesting way to ensure cross-pollination. The flowers of some plants have long male parts (stamens) that fill the upper flower tube, concealing shorter female parts (stigma and style) at the base. On other plants, a long style projects from the flower tube, with short stamens below. When insects carry pollen from flower to flower, they leave the pollen from long-stamened flowers on the stigmas of only short-stamened flowers, and vice versa. • The name *Houstonia* honours William Houston, an 18th-century Scottish botanist and surgeon. *H. longifolia* has also been called *Hedyotis longifolia*.

Plant: tufted perennial 6–25 cm tall, with many erect, 4-sided, often purplish stems
Leaves: paired, narrowly oblong, 1–3 cm long, 1-nerved, stalkless, with 2 small, whitish to purplish stipules at the base
Flowers: purplish to pink or white, funnel-shaped, hairy inside, 6–9 mm long, with 4 spreading petal lobes and 4 slender sepals; many flowers in leafy, branched, flat-topped clusters **Blooms:** May to September
Fruits: egg-shaped capsules, splitting open across the top **Habitat:** open, sandy sites
Distribution: native from Quebec to Alberta to Florida **Pick:** none

Northern Bedstraw

Galium boreale

This herb belongs to the same family as coffee, and its tiny nutlets can be roasted as a coffee substitute. The name bedstraw refers to the historical use of European plants as a fragrant stuffing for mattresses and pillows. Young plants are edible, but more often bedstraw has been used as medicine, often in hot poultices to stop bleeding and reduce swelling. The plant juice has been applied alone or in salves to heal sunburn, rashes, cuts, insect bites, eczema, ringworm and other skin problems. Northern bedstraw tea was traditionally taken to relieve diarrhea, bladder infections and kidney stones, but more recently it has been promoted as a weight-loss aid. Continued use, however, can irritate the mouth and tongue.

Plant: erect, leafy perennial 20–80 cm tall, with simple or branched, smooth, 4-angled stems **Leaves:** in circles (whorls) of 4; narrow, 3-nerved, 1.5–4.5 cm long, stalkless **Flowers:** white or creamy, 3.5–7 mm across, with 4 spreading petal lobes; many flowers in showy, branched clusters **Blooms:** June to August **Fruits:** pairs of seed-like nutlets 2 mm long **Habitat:** variable, but not too dry **Distribution:** native from Quebec to Alaska and around the world **Pick:** a few

Blue Giant-Hyssop
Agastache foeniculum

This tall, leafy plant, with its pleasant anise-like fragrance, has often been used for food and medicine. Young plants provide cooked greens and flavouring for soups and stews. The fresh flowers add splashes of purple to salads and cooked dishes. Fresh or dried leaves, covered with boiling water and steeped or simmered, produce a delicately licorice-flavoured tea. The leaves also add flavour to commercial teas. Cooled giant-hyssop leaf tea is still drunk occasionally to relieve coughs and chest pains. It has been credited with curing dispirited hearts and inducing sweating. • This robust, common mint could prove to be a source of essential oil for perfume and aromatherapy. It is easily grown from seeds, cuttings or root divisions, especially on sandy, limy, well-drained soil in sunny sites. The flower clusters dry well and look beautiful in dried floral arrangements.

Plant: erect perennial 30–100 cm tall, with 4-sided stems from creeping rootstock
Leaves: paired, whitish underneath with fine, close hairs, ovate, 2–7 cm long, coarsely toothed, short-stalked
Flowers: blue, funnel-shaped, 2-lipped, 6–12 mm long, with a blue, hairy, 5-lobed calyx; flowers in dense, usually interrupted spikes 2–10 cm long **Blooms:** July to August **Fruits:** 4 small nutlets within the calyx **Habitat:** well-drained, open sites **Distribution:** native from Quebec to Alberta to the central U.S. **Pick:** a few

Tall Meadow-Rue

Thalictrum dasycarpum

Tall meadow-rue produces blooms in abundance. Although the flowers are small and lack petals, they form conspicuous, showy clusters on tall stems. Each plant is either male or female. The males are easily recognized by their clusters of dangling stamens, whereas the females are less showy at first but develop distinctive heads of small fruits later in summer. • In the first century AD, the Roman scholar Pliny recommended meadow-rue for preventing baldness and restoring hair. Since then, these plants have seldom been used as medicine. Most species, however, produce chemicals called alkaloids, some of which have been used to combat tumours. A few species contain the heart toxin thalictrine. • Meadow-rue seeds and leaves remain fragrant when dried and make a nice addition to sachets for scenting clothing drawers and linen cupboards.

Plant: leafy, often purplish perennial 1–2 m tall **Leaves:** 3–4 times divided in threes; leaflets 3-lobed **Flowers:** pale yellow to purplish, with 4–5 slender sepals (no petals); male and female flowers usually on separate plants in leafy, pyramid-shaped clusters; anthers 1.5–3.5 mm long **Blooms:** June to July **Fruits:** 6–8-ribbed, seed-like achenes 4–6 mm long, in hemispherical heads **Habitat:** wet, open sites **Distribution:** native from Ontario to Alberta, south to Missouri and Oklahoma **Pick:** a few

Curly Dock
Rumex crispus

Tart, lemony dock leaves make a flavourful addition to stews, soups and stir-fries, but they can become distinctly bitter with age. In moderation, the tender young leaves add zing to salads and sandwiches. Like its cousin common rhubarb *(Rheum rhabarbarum)*, curly dock contains oxalic acid, which is toxic in large quantities, but heating and freezing can both destroy this toxin. The seeds were pounded into meal or roasted as a coffee substitute. The fleshy winter roots were collected during spring plowing and cooked as a vegetable. Dried, powdered roots provided a tooth-brushing powder. Some herbalists use dock as a liver stimulant, blood cleanser and mild laxative.
• This prolific immigrant is a naturalized weed around the world. Each plant can produce more than 60,000 seeds that are able to survive for up to 80 years.

Plant: erect perennial 50–150 cm tall, from taproot **Leaves:** lance-shaped, 10–30 cm long, with finely rippled edges and rounded to notched bases **Flowers:** green or pinkish, with 3 tiny sepals and 3 larger inner flaps (valves); flowers in circles (whorls) in narrow, branched clusters 10–40 cm long **Blooms:** April to July **Fruits:** 3-sided, seed-like achenes enclosed by 3 papery, golden to red-brown, 5 mm long valves, each with a conspicuous wart-like bump
Habitat: moist, often disturbed sites
Distribution: Eurasia; naturalized across Canada and the U.S. **Pick:** freely

Common Pepper-Grass
Lepidium densiflorum

Like many weeds in the mustard family, common pepper-grass was traditionally used for food. In spring, the pleasant, peppery, tender young plants added zest to sandwiches, salads, stews and casseroles. The leaves are rich in minerals and vitamins (especially vitamin C), so they could cure scurvy in spring and on ocean voyages. Pepper-grass pods, with their stronger mustard flavour, make an interesting addition to soups and stews. The dried pods can be stored for year-round use. Their cylindrical clusters make an eye-catching addition to dried-flower arrangements.
• This common wayside weed is usually recognized by its seed pods, rather than by its inconspicuous flowers. A single plant can produce up to 5000 seeds. As contaminants in crop seed and in feed, pepper-grass seeds have carried the plant to roadsides, planted fields and settlements across the continent.
• Common pepper-grass has also been called miner's pepperwort.

Plant: erect, greyish annual or winter-annual 15–60 cm tall, with freely branched stems from taproot **Leaves:** narrowly lance-shaped, 3–10 cm long, toothed or lobed **Flowers:** greenish, inconspicuous, cross-shaped, about 2 mm across, with 4 petals (often absent) and 4 sepals; numerous flowers in elongating, cylindrical clusters 5–15 cm long **Blooms:** April to June
Fruits: hairless, flattened, ovate pods 2–3.5 mm long, with notched tips, containing 2 seeds
Habitat: dry, open, often disturbed sites
Distribution: native from Newfoundland to Alaska to Texas, and introduced from Europe
Pick: freely

Wormseed Wallflower

Erysimum cheiranthoides

The intensely bitter seeds of this plant were once given to children to clear obstructions and flush parasites from the intestines, hence 'wormseed' in the common name. Small doses induced vomiting and diarrhea, but large doses were quite toxic. In North America, various tribes boiled the roots to make washes for healing sores. • All parts of this plant, and especially the seeds, contain toxic mustard oils. Most livestock refuse to eat the pungent, bitter-tasting seed or any feed contaminated with it. • Wormseed wallflower is rarely a problem in cultivated fields, but it can be difficult to control in tame-mustard crops such as canola. It spreads readily, with each plant producing up to 3500 seeds. Most colonies of this common weed are direct descendants of plants that were brought from Europe.

Plant: slightly hairy annual with parallel, flat-lying, T-shaped hairs on erect stems 20–60 cm tall, from taproot **Leaves:** slender to lance-shaped, 2–8 cm long, with flat-lying, 3-pronged hairs **Flowers:** yellow, cross-shaped, 3–5 mm across, on slender, spreading stalks; flowers in dense, rounded, elongating clusters **Blooms:** June to August **Fruits:** slender, erect to ascending, nearly hairless, 4-sided pods 1–3 cm long and 1 mm thick **Habitat:** moist, disturbed sites **Distribution:** introduced (mainly; from Eurasia) and native from Newfoundland to Alaska to Florida and California, and around the world **Pick:** freely

Tumbleweed Mustard

Sisymbrium altissimum

This successful immigrant is native to the western Mediterranean region and northern Africa. Early settlers and Native peoples sometimes used its small seeds for seasoning, and a few tribes boiled the ground seed to make gruel. Tumbleweed mustard makes a good potherb, but only when the leaves are young and tender, before the plant flowers. Try adding a few young leaves to salads and soups. • Tumbleweed mustard will occasionally infest fields, but it is not usually considered a noxious weed. A single plant can produce up to 2700 seeds. In fall, the dried skeletons of dead plants form airy spheres that break off near the ground and tumble freely in the wind, scattering seeds along the way. • Tumbleweed mustard is also called tall hedge-mustard.

Plant: essentially hairless annual (sometimes biennial) 30–100 cm tall, much branched above **Leaves:** stalked, deeply pinnately cut into slender, often toothed lobes; upper leaves skeleton-like **Flowers:** pale yellow, about 6–14 mm across, cross-shaped, with 4 petals and 4 sepals; flowers borne at branch tips in elongating clusters **Blooms:** June to August **Fruits:** slender, ascending to spreading pods 5–10 cm long, 1–1.5 mm wide, with stalks almost as thick **Habitat:** disturbed ground **Distribution:** Europe; naturalized across North America **Pick:** freely

Wild Mustard

Sinapis arvensis

Wild mustard was brought to North America as a source of cooking greens, mustard seasoning and burning oil. Unfortunately, it is now regarded mainly as a noxious weed. A single plant may produce 3500 seeds, which can survive for up to 60 years, germinating when conditions permit. • Many significant crops, including canola and other rapeseed varieties, turnip, cabbage, cauliflower, kale and brown mustard, are species of the genus *Brassica* and are closely related to wild mustard. As a result, wild mustard can be very difficult to identify and control when it invades fields of some of these crops. Not only does wild mustard compete for moisture and nutrients, but its seeds reduce the quality of the oil when mixed with canola. • *S. arvensis* has also been called *Brassica kaber*.

Plant: coarse annual with bristly stems 20–80 cm tall, from slender taproot
Leaves: widest above midleaf, coarsely toothed to lobed, 5–20 cm long
Flowers: yellow, 1.5 cm across, cross-shaped, with 4 petals and 4 sepals; flowers on stout, ascending stalks in elongating clusters **Blooms:** May to July
Fruits: 3–5-nerved, cylindrical pods 1.5–4 cm long, tipped with a 4-sided (sometimes 1-seeded) beak about half as long as the pod **Habitat:** waste places, fields **Distribution:** Eurasia; naturalized across North America **Pick:** freely

Buck-Bean

Menyanthes trifoliata

In Europe, powdered buck-bean roots were mixed with flour as a nutritious but bitter bread additive. This practice was especially common in times of famine. More commonly, the bitter leaves were used as a substitute for hops in flavouring beer and were also boiled in honey to make mead. Buck-bean has also been used medicinally for jaundice, indigestion, skin diseases, scurvy, intestinal worms and rheumatism. None of these uses has been proved effective, though the strong-tasting bitters may help stimulate appetite. • Some people recommend buck-bean leaf as a pleasantly bitter addition to summer salads and cream-cheese sandwiches, but only in small amounts. Larger servings cause vomiting and diarrhea.

Plant: fleshy, hairless perennial 10–30 cm tall, from coarse rootstock **Leaves:** basal, long-stalked, divided into 3 leaflets 3–8 cm long, with smooth or wavy edges **Flowers:** white, usually purple-tinged, funnel-shaped, about 2 cm across, with 5 spreading, hairy petals; 10–20 flowers in elongating clusters held just above the water **Blooms:** May to July **Fruits:** thick-walled, egg-shaped capsules 6–9 mm long **Habitat:** standing water **Distribution:** native from Newfoundland to Alaska to the southwestern U.S. and around the world **Pick:** none

Arum-Leaved Arrowhead

Sagittaria cuneata

Although this species is smaller than its better-known cousin wapato *(S. latifolia)*, its fleshy tubers are equally edible. The tubers lie underwater, buried in mud and some distance from the stem, so Native women had to feel around with their toes in icy water to find them. When the miniature 'potatoes' were dislodged, they bobbed to the surface and were skimmed into containers. • Wapato tubers can be 4–5 cm across, but those of arum-leaved arrowhead are much smaller. It takes a lot of energy to gather enough to make a meal, so despite their pleasant flavour (once cooked), these tiny tubers were rarely used. • This common aquatic plant is a valuable source of food for waterfowl and muskrats. People have sometimes raided muskrat push-ups to steal caches of the tasty tubers.

Plant: aquatic perennial; stems 20–50 cm long, from spreading rootstock with fleshy tubers
Leaves: arrowhead-shaped, 1–12 cm long, with the 2 lobes shorter than upper blade; submerged leaves slender, up to 40 cm long **Flowers:** waxy white, about 1 cm across, with 3 petals and 3 sepals; flowers usually in whorls of 3 in elongating clusters with female whorls below male
Blooms: June to August **Fruits:** seed-like achenes, in 1 cm heads **Habitat:** shallow water and muddy shores **Distribution:** native from Labrador to Alaska to Texas **Pick:** none

Common Blue-Eyed-Grass

Sisyrinchium montanum

The cheerful blue eyes of this dainty wildflower often seem to float among blades of grass. Without the sun, the flower petals close, and this slender plant disappears among its grassy neighbours. • Common blue-eyed-grass isn't a grass at all. Believe it or not, it belongs to the iris family. Try running your fingers along the stems. You'll discover that these stems are distinctly two-sided, not round like those of grass. Also, the leaves attach edgewise to the stem, just like those of a true iris (genus *Iris*). • A few tribes added this plant to medicinal teas for diarrhea, worms and stomachaches, but common blue-eyed-grass hasn't been widely used. The seeds can take more than two years to germinate, so these delicate blue blossoms seldom peek out from flowerbeds.

Plant: slender, clumped perennial 10–50 cm tall, with unbranched, flattened, narrow-winged stems 1–4 mm wide
Leaves: grass-like, 1–3.5 mm wide
Flowers: bright violet blue, star-shaped, 6–10 mm across, with 6 abruptly pointed or notched tepals; flowers single or in small clusters from between two 1–6 cm bracts at stem tips **Blooms:** late May to July **Fruits:** round, 3–6 mm capsules on thread-like stalks **Habitat:** moist, open sites **Distribution:** native from Newfoundland to the Yukon, south to North Carolina and Texas **Pick:** a few

Starry False-Solomon's-Seal

Maianthemum stellatum

This graceful wildflower is named for its delicate, star-shaped flowers. 'Solomon's-seal' refers to a six-pointed star like the Star of David, and *stellatum* means 'star-like.' • Although the berries can taste sweet, large amounts cause vomiting and diarrhea when eaten raw. The rootstocks were sometimes used for food, but usually they had to be soaked in lye to remove the bitterness, and then washed and boiled to remove the lye. Like onions, these fleshy roots were used to flavour other foods. • Medicinally, the roots were chewed raw or used in syrups and teas to relieve coughs. They were also applied as poultices to burns and swellings. The young leaves and shoots are said to be edible, but this lovely plant should be gathered only in an emergency. • This species has also been called *Smilacina stellata*.

Plant: erect perennial 20–60 cm tall, from rootstock **Leaves:** alternate on zigzagged stems, oblong to lance-shaped, 6–15 cm long, usually folded, sometimes clasping **Flowers:** white, 8–10 mm across, with 6 oblong tepals; flowers in elongating, 2–5 cm clusters **Blooms:** May to June **Fruits:** 6–10 mm berries, green with 6 dark stripes at first, blackish red when mature
Habitat: moist woods, shores and meadows **Distribution:** native from Newfoundland to Alaska, south through the U.S. **Pick:** none

White Death-Camas

Zigadenus elegans

Beware! All parts of this rather innocent-looking wildflower contain toxic chemicals (alkaloids) said to be more potent than strychnine. Sheep (particularly), cattle, horses and chickens have been poisoned by *Zigadenus* species, with losses of up to 2000 animals at a time. Human deaths have usually occurred when the bulbs were mistaken for those of a wild onion (*Allium* spp.) or camas (*Camassia* spp). Just two bulbs can be fatal. Symptoms include salivating, vomiting, diarrhea, lowered body temperature and a slow heartbeat. If you think that someone has eaten these bulbs, encourage vomiting and get the person to a doctor as soon as possible. • *Zigadenus* means 'yoked glands,' referring to the two-lobed gland on each petal. This genus name has also been spelled *Zygadenus*.

Plant: erect perennial 20–60 cm tall, from an onion-like bulb **Leaves:** grass-like, blue-green, mostly basal, up to 1.2 cm wide, with parallel veins **Flowers:** white to greenish white, star-shaped, with 6 oblong, 7–12 mm long tepals each bearing a green, heart-shaped gland near the base; flowers in branched clusters 10–30 cm long **Blooms:** July to August **Fruits:** egg-shaped, 1–1.5 cm long capsules containing angular, 3 mm seeds **Habitat:** moist to wet, open sites **Distribution:** native from Quebec to Alaska, south to Mexico **Pick:** none (abundant, but toxic)

Wood Lily

Lilium philadelphicum

This bright orange wildflower creates splashes of colour along waysides across Canada. It is Saskatchewan's floral emblem. • Many tribes gathered the bulbs of wood lily for food and medicine. The bulbs are said to have an excellent flavour, either raw or cooked. As well, the abundant, nutritious pollen can be dusted on various dishes. Medicinally, the bulbs were once cooked and then applied to sores, bruises, swellings or wounds. They were also used to make a tea for treating stomach problems, coughs and fevers and for helping women in labour to deliver the afterbirth. • Wood lilies have disappeared from many populated places. Picking the flowers with their leafy stems or gathering the bulbs kills these beautiful plants. Please leave them for others to enjoy.

Plant: erect perennial 30–90 cm tall, from bulb 2–3 cm thick **Leaves:** slender, 3–10 cm long, rough-edged, in circles (whorls) of 3–8 upwards on the stem, often alternate below **Flowers:** usually reddish orange (red to yellowish), with 6 purple-spotted tepals, broadly funnel-shaped, 6–10 cm long, held erect; 1–5 flowers per plant **Blooms:** June to August **Fruits:** oblong capsules 4–7 cm long, with packed rows of flat seeds **Habitat:** dry woods, meadows, roadsides **Distribution:** native from Quebec to B.C., south to New Mexico **Pick:** none

Yellow Pond-Lily

Nuphar lutea

Long, slender stalks anchor these floating flowers and leaves to deeply buried rootstocks. The stalks contain large air-filled tubes that carry oxygen to the roots and waste gases to the surface. • Native peoples gathered the thick rootstocks in winter and spring, boiled or roasted them for several hours, then peeled them to expose their sweet, gluey contents. Rootstocks were also sliced, dried and ground into meal or flour. The starchy seeds can be difficult to remove, so some tribes rotted the fruits to soften them. The heated seeds swell like poor-quality popcorn, making a crunchy snack. • This species includes *N. variegata*.

Plant: aquatic perennial from large rootstock
Leaves: floating (sometimes underwater), round-heart-shaped, 7–35 cm long, on long, narrowly winged stalks **Flowers:** single, cupped, 3.5–6 cm across, with about 6 yellow, petal-like sepals (often reddish inside) and many large (4–7 mm) anthers around a yellowish, 1 cm disc (stigma) with about 10–15 lines radiating from the centre
Blooms: May to September **Fruits:** egg-shaped, spongy to leathery berries 2–4.5 cm long
Habitat: quiet waters **Distribution:** native across North America **Pick:** none

Yellow Marsh-Marigold
Caltha palustris

Bright yellow clumps of this shining flower brighten many dark, damp hollows in spring and early summer. Although the buttercup-like blooms appear evenly yellow to human eyes, their petal tips reflect ultraviolet light and their bases absorb it. As a result, insects such as bees, whose eyes detect ultraviolet light, see distinct patterns that direct them to nectaries at the centre of the flower. • Yellow marsh-marigold is sometimes grown as an ornamental in moist, shady gardens. This rather toxic plant has also been used for food and medicine, but it contains strong irritants that can cause blistering, and it is poisonous if eaten raw.

Plant: fleshy perennial 20–60 cm tall, with thick, hollow stems **Leaves:** dark green, heart-shaped to kidney-shaped, 5–17 cm long, shallowly toothed, smaller and more widely notched upwards on the stem **Flowers:** bright, shiny yellow, saucer-shaped, 1.5–4 cm across, with 5–9 petal-like sepals (no petals), 50–120 stamens and a dense cluster of pistils; flowers in branched clusters **Blooms:** April to June **Fruits:** capsules (follicles) 1–1.5 cm long, borne in head-like clusters **Habitat:** wet sites, often in shallow water **Distribution:** native across North America and around the world **Pick:** none; caution

Meadow Buttercup

Ranunculus acris

Some sources suggest meadow buttercup as a lovely addition to the garden, but unsuspecting gardeners will likely find themselves fighting to keep this prolific European weed at bay. • The specific epithet *acris* describes the acrid sap of this buttercup. The caustic, bitter juice discourages browsers, but it can also blister sensitive skin. • The characteristic shininess of these flowers comes from a specialized film of white cells in the petals that reflects light. Tall stems hold the bright yellow blooms above surrounding plants to attract the attention of pollinating insects. • Meadow buttercup has also been called tall buttercup.

Plant: slender, branched perennial 60–100 cm tall **Leaves:** kidney-shaped, divided into wedge-shaped, deeply lobed parts arranged like fingers on a hand (palmate) **Flowers:** glossy yellow, saucer-shaped, about 2.5 cm across, with 5 broadly ovate petals, 5 greenish, spreading sepals and many stamens and pistils; few to several flowers in loose clusters **Blooms:** May to September **Fruits:** flattened, seed-like achenes 2–3 mm long, with a 0.4–1 mm beak; achenes in round heads **Habitat:** meadows and disturbed habitats **Distribution:** Europe; naturalized across North America **Pick:** freely; caution

Canada Anemone

Anemone canadensis

This common wildflower is easily identified by the circle of coarsely toothed, stalkless leaves high on its flower stems. Anemone flowers have no true petals. Instead, the five showy sepals attract pollinating insects. • In the western U.S., some tribes attributed mystical powers to Canada anemone and valued its roots as medicine, applied in washes and poultices. However, anemones contain many of the caustic substances that are common in species of the buttercup family, so handle these plants with care, especially if you have sensitive skin. • Another common name for anemone is windflower. The genus name comes from the Greek *anemos*, 'wind,' because these beautiful flowers were thought to open with the first breezes of spring.

Plant: erect perennial 20–80 cm tall, from spreading rootstock **Leaves:** cut into 3–5 sharply toothed parts, long-stalked at the plant base and stalkless in a circle below the flowers **Flowers:** white, saucer-shaped, 2.5–3.8 cm across, with 5 petal-like sepals (no petals); flowers single or sometimes 2–3 **Blooms:** May to August **Fruits:** seed-like achenes 3–5 mm long, flattened, with flat-lying hairs; achenes in round heads **Habitat:** moist, open sites **Distribution:** native across temperate North America **Pick:** a few; caution

Prairie-Crocus

Pulsatilla patens

What better floral emblem for Manitoba than this hardy harbinger of spring? Prairie-crocuses often push their way up through snow, spreading a blanket of mauve across the prairie. • Prairie-crocuses may appear delicate, but they are best left alone. Their sap can blister sensitive skin and cause vomiting, tremors and even collapse if any parts are eaten. Most animals avoid eating these caustic plants, so fields of prairie-crocus can be a sign of overgrazing. Even the juice of the purple flowers can irritate, but it was sometimes used to colour Easter eggs—hence the alternative name pasqueflower for the Paschal or Easter season. • *P. patens* has also been called crocus anemone, *P. ludoviciana* and *Anemone patens*.

Plant: tufted, silky-hairy perennial 10–40 cm tall
Leaves: mainly basal, 4–10 cm wide, divided 1–3 times into slender segments, long stalked; stem leaves smaller, in a ring near midstem, stalkless
Flowers: blue to purple (rarely white), cupped, about 2.5–3.5 cm across, with 5–7 petal-like sepals (no true petals); single **Blooms:** March to June
Fruits: silky-hairy, seed-like achenes tipped with a feathery style 2–4 cm long; achenes in fluffy heads when mature **Habitat:** open, well-drained sites
Distribution: native from western Ontario to Alaska, south through the U.S. **Pick:** a few; caution

Northern Grass-of-Parnassus

Parnassia palustris

This innocent-looking little flower is one of nature's tricksters. Its delicate white blooms have a ring of yellowish green structures called staminodia near their centres. Each staminodium has 7 to 15 slender fingers, each tipped with a shiny knob that mimics a drop of nectar. Small flies flock to this apparent sweet feast. After landing, they are guided to the centre of the flower by prominent pale green or yellow veins on the petals. Having been fooled by the staminodia, they don't bother eating the real stamens, but they do brush past them, picking up loads of pollen. A few days later, the stamens fade, and the stigmas then become sticky and ready to receive the pollen carried by insects arriving from other blossoms. • Northern grass-of-Parnassus has also been called marsh grass-of-Parnassus.

Plant: hairless perennial 10–30 cm tall
Leaves: mainly basal, heart-shaped, 0.5–2 cm long, stalked; stem leaf single, heart-shaped, clasping lower stem
Flowers: white, saucer-shaped, about 2 cm across, with 5 sepals, 5 petals, 5 fertile stamens, 5 staminodia (sterile stamens) and an egg-shaped ovary; single
Blooms: July to August **Fruits:** many-seeded capsules 8–12 mm long
Habitat: moist, open or shaded sites
Distribution: native from Newfoundland to Alaska, south through the western U.S. and around the world **Pick:** a few

Beeplant
Cleome serrulata

This lovely, nectar-rich wild-flower is sometimes culti-vated as a source of nectar for honeybees. The sweet, pink blossoms are edible, and the seeds have been used as spice, but the plant itself has an unpleasant smell and taste. Still, many people have eaten beeplant over the years, and it is even reported to have saved lives during famines. Long boiling with a change of water helped reduce the strong odour and flavour. Cooked bee-plant was eaten with cornmeal porridge, added to stews or rolled into balls and fried. Sometimes these balls were dried for later use. • Those who didn't want to eat their beeplant found other ways to use it. With patient boil-ing, plants could be reduced to a thick paste that served as a black paint or dye. • Beeplant has also been called spiderflower.

Plant: erect annual 25–100 cm tall, with branched stems from taproot
Leaves: divided into 3 slender leaflets 1.5–7 cm long **Flowers:** reddish purple to pale pink, cross-shaped, about 2 cm across; in head-like clusters that elongate with age **Blooms:** May to August
Fruits: cylindrical pods 3–6 cm long, spreading to nodding on 1–2 cm stalks
Habitat: open, disturbed sites
Distribution: native from Quebec to B.C., south through the U.S. **Pick:** a few

Field Mouse-Ear-Chickweed

Cerastium arvense

This showy little wildflower can carpet the ground with masses of delicate white flowers. Unfortunately, its efforts aren't always appreciated. Field mouse-ear-chickweed has been designated a weed in Manitoba and Alberta. Although it cannot tolerate plowing and so is not a problem in cultivated fields, it thrives on lawns and in overgrazed pastures. • If you'd like to cultivate this native species, you shouldn't have trouble growing it from seed, which is abundant, or from plant divisions. • Field mouse-ear-chickweed is edible, but its hairiness and small size limit its appeal. Usually it is cooked before it is eaten. • Given its preferred habitat, the name *arvense*, 'of the fields,' is very appropriate.

Plant: grey-green, hairy, sometimes glandular perennial 10–30 cm tall, with tufted or matted stems
Leaves: paired, 1-nerved, awl-shaped to lance-shaped, 1–4 cm long; main leaf axils usually with small clusters of leaves or short sterile shoots
Flowers: white, broadly funnel-shaped, 1–2 cm across, with 5 broad, 2-lobed petals and 5 small sepals; few to many flowers on slender, 1–3 cm stalks in open clusters **Blooms:** May to July
Fruits: curved, cylindrical capsules up to 1.2 cm long, containing golden to reddish brown, bumpy seeds
Habitat: dry, open sites **Distribution:** native from Newfoundland to Alaska to Georgia and New Mexico and around the world **Pick:** freely

Bladder Campion

Silene vulgaris

Historically, bladder campion saved lives by providing survival food for the people of Minorca when swarms of locusts destroyed the harvest in 1685. The young leaves, with their sweet, pea-like flavour, were once popular in Europe as a spring potherb. However, the plant becomes very bitter and unpleasant with age as the soap (saponin) content increases. • Bladder campion is a common weed but not a serious problem in planted fields. It produces exquisite urn-shaped capsules that appear to be made of polished wood. These capsules make an interesting addition to dried-flower arrangements. • *S. vulgaris* has also been called *S. cucubalus*.

Plant: bluish green perennial 20–80 cm tall, from deep roots **Leaves:** paired, ovate, 3–10 cm long, often clasping, sometimes fringed **Flowers:** whitish, with 5 white, deeply 2-lobed, 3.5–6 mm wide petal blades sticking out from a papery, grey-green to purple-tinged balloon of fused sepals about 1 cm across; flowers in clusters of 5–30 **Blooms:** April to August **Fruits:** 3-chambered capsules opening by 6 teeth; enclosed in sepal balloons 1–2 cm across **Habitat:** disturbed ground **Distribution:** Europe; naturalized across North America **Pick:** freely

Scarlet Globe-Mallow

Sphaeralcea coccinea

Globe-mallow plants contain lots of mucilage, so they are very slimy inside. The leaves were chewed or crushed to make cooling poultices, used for soothing sores, wounds, inflamed skin and blistered feet. The flowers and leaves were chewed or made into tea for relieving upset stomachs and sore throats. This pleasant drink was also used as a tonic to improve appetite and sweeten bitter medicines. In some tribes, spiritual leaders chewed scarlet globe-mallow plants into paste that they rubbed onto their skin for protection from scalding. With this shield they were said to amaze spectators by reaching into boiling kettles for chunks of hot meat. • *S. coccinea* has also been called *Malvastrum coccineum*.

Plant: low perennial 10–20 cm tall, with dense, star-shaped hairs **Leaves:** yellowish green, grey-hairy underneath, deeply cut into 3–5 wedge-shaped, 2–5 cm long segments arranged like fingers on a hand (palmate) **Flowers:** orange to brick red, 1–2 cm across, with 5 broad, shallowly notched petals and 5 small sepals; flowers in compact clusters at stem tips **Blooms:** May to August **Fruits:** hairy discs composed of many 1-seeded segments, resembling wedges in a wheel of cheese **Habitat:** dry, open sites **Distribution:** native from Manitoba to Alberta, south through the U.S. **Pick:** a few

Fringed Yellow-Loosestrife

Lysimachia ciliata

The name 'loosestrife' suggests that this pretty little wildflower should relieve tension, but instead it often creates confusion. Some say *Lysimachia* comes from the Greek *lysis*, or 'loosening,' and *machê*, 'strife,' because it calmed unruly oxen when hung from their yokes. Others believe the name honours the ancient King Lysimachus of Thrace, who discovered its medicinal powers—though it's not at all clear what those powers are. To add to the confusion, the name *Lysimachia* once referred to both a yellow-flowered plant (now called *L. vulgaris*) and a purple-flowered plant (now *Lythrum salicaria*, p. 135). Plants of both genera have kept the common name 'loosestrife' even though they aren't even distantly related. • *L. ciliata* is also known by the name *Steironema ciliata*.

Plant: erect perennial 30–130 cm tall, from creeping underground rootstock
Leaves: paired, roughly ovate, 4–14 cm long, with prominently fringed stalks
Flowers: yellow, 1.5–2.5 cm across, saucer-shaped, with 5 abruptly slender-pointed petals, 5 sepals, 5 fertile stamens, 5 sterile stamens and 1 style; flowers borne on slender, 1.5–6.5 cm stalks from leaf axils **Blooms:** June to August **Fruits:** small, rounded capsules **Habitat:** moist to wet sites **Distribution:** native from Quebec to B.C., Alaska, southern U.S. **Pick:** a few

Three-Flowered Avens

Geum triflorum

Settlers affectionately called three-flowered avens colourful names such as 'old man's whiskers' or 'prairie smoke.' The fluffy fruiting heads looked like the wispy beard of an old man, and when plants grew in profusion they spread a smoke-like haze across the prairie. • A pleasant tea, made from the fragrant pink roots, was widely used as a beverage and also as a medicine for treating colds, flu and fevers. Avens plants are astringent and therefore cause soft tissues to pucker. Because of this, the root tea can reduce bleeding and inflammation, so it was used to treat diarrhea and dysentery and to soothe sore eyes, mouths and throats. In the sweathouse, the roots were boiled to make a purifying wash for relieving aches and pains.

Plant: reddish, soft-hairy perennial 10–30 cm tall, from stout rootstock **Leaves:** mainly basal, 5–20 cm long, pinnately divided into many toothed or lobed leaflets **Flowers:** purplish to dusty pink, urn-shaped, about 2 cm across, nodding; in loose clusters of 3 (sometimes 1–9) **Blooms:** May to July **Fruits:** seed-like achenes 3 mm long, tipped with a feathery, 2–4 cm bristle (the elongated style); fruits form erect, fluffy heads **Habitat:** open, well-drained sites **Distribution:** native from Ontario to B.C., south through the western U.S. **Pick:** a few

Yellow Avens

Geum aleppicum

This widespread plant has been used for medicine all around the world. North American Native peoples boiled the roots to make teas for treating coughs, sore mouths and throats, chest congestion, diarrhea and fever. In China, it was used to treat bug bites, convulsions, fever, nervous irritability, skin diseases and painful sores and wounds. • Large clumps of yellow avens make a showy addition to wildflower gardens, but beware of the burs. Each blossom produces a bristling head of tiny, clinging fruits that latch onto passersby. These very persistent hangers-on led to the Cree name 'jealousy plant,' and because of this clinging quality, men used yellow avens as a love charm. Women who were thus afflicted mixed it into their antidotes.

Plant: erect, coarse-hairy perennial 40–100 cm tall, from short rootstock **Leaves:** mainly basal, pinnately divided into 5–7 main leaflets interspersed with smaller leaflets; tip leaflet largest, tapered to a wedge-shaped base **Flowers:** bright yellow, saucer-shaped, 1–2.5 cm across, with 5 petals and 5 sepals; flowers in open, flat-topped clusters **Blooms:** June to July **Fruits:** hairy, seed-like achenes 3–4 mm long, tipped with a hooked 4–6 mm bristle; fruits in bur-like heads 1–1.5 cm wide **Habitat:** moist sites **Distribution:** native from Quebec to Alaska to Georgia and New Mexico, and around the world **Pick:** a few

Common Silverweed

Argentina anserina

This charming little 'rose' often forms carpets of silver and green leaves dotted with sunny yellow flowers. Although it is easily overlooked, common silverweed is a circumpolar plant with an interesting history. In western Scotland, its starchy roots are said to have saved entire villages from starvation during famines. Raw, boiled or roasted, the spring roots have been likened to parsnips, chestnuts and sweet potatoes. Medicinally, common silverweed was used mainly as an astringent in gargles, washes and teas for reducing inflammation and stopping bleeding of the digestive tract, kidneys and skin. • *A. anserina* has also been called *Potentilla anserina*.

Plant: low perennial with slender, creeping runners **Leaves:** basal, up to 30 cm long, silvery-hairy and woolly underneath, pinnately divided into many sharply toothed leaflets with small and large leaflets interspersed **Flowers:** yellow, 1.5–2.5 cm across, with 5 petals above 5 sepals and 5 smaller, alternating bractlets; flowers single **Blooms:** May to September **Fruits:** thick, furrowed, seed-like achenes 2.5 mm long, in dense heads **Habitat:** well-drained to wet, open sites **Distribution:** native across North America and around the world **Pick:** a few

Plains Cinquefoil
Potentilla bipinnatifida

The name *Potentilla*, from *potens*, 'potent,' refers to cinquefoils' supposed medicinal powers, especially their ability to stop bleeding and diarrhea in both man and beast. But despite their name, *Potentilla* species are not widely used for medicine. Like most members of the rose family, these plants contain tannins, which constrict soft tissues, but other astringent medicines are generally preferred. Cinquefoil tea has been used occasionally to treat fevers, diarrhea and mouth or throat infections. Young leaves produce a pleasant, golden, calcium-rich tea, but the plants soon become quite bitter. • Tannin-rich cinquefoils have also been used to tan hides and to give leather a beautiful reddish colour. With a chrome mordant, the crushed roots dye wool red-brown, and with iron the wool takes on a purplish red hue. The flowers make a bright yellow dye.

Plant: clumped, usually hairy, erect perennial 20–50 cm tall, from stout root crown
Leaves: grey-green above, white-woolly underneath, about 10–25 cm long, long-stalked, pinnately divided into 3–7 leaflets (sometimes appearing palmate); leaflets 3–6 cm long, deeply cut into 1.5–3 mm wide lobes **Flowers:** yellow, 6–10 mm across, with 5 small petals, 5 conspicuous sepals (longer than petals) and 5 smaller alternating bractlets; flowers in branched clusters **Blooms:** July to August **Fruits:** seed-like achenes 1 mm long **Habitat:** dry, open sites **Distribution:** native from Newfoundland to Alaska to New Hampshire and Arizona **Pick:** a few

White Cinquefoil
Potentilla arguta

This tall wildflower lifts its blooms above surrounding plants to catch the attention of potential pollinators. When an insect lands, it immediately moves in a circle around the top of the flower, gathering nectar on its tongue and pollen on its feet. In a few seconds the visitor moves on to another bloom.

• Once a flower is pollinated, its bracts and sepals fold upwards into a tight bundle with the developing seeds protected inside. When the seeds ripen, these outer layers loosen slightly, and as the tall stems sway in the breeze, they scatter the seeds over the ground. In winter, the clusters of urn-shaped heads add variety to dried bouquets.

• Abundant hairs trap moist air on the surface of leaves and stems, helping this prairie plant conserve water.

• The large genus *Potentilla* includes more than 200 species in the Northern Hemisphere. White cinquefoil has also been called tall cinquefoil.

Plant: glandular-hairy perennial 30–100 cm tall, from short rootstock **Leaves:** long-stalked, pinnately divided into 7–11 leaflets; leaflets egg-shaped, coarsely sharp-toothed, 1.5–4 cm long **Flowers:** white to cream-coloured, saucer-shaped, 1.2–1.8 cm across, with 5 petals above 5 sepals alternating with 5 slender bractlets; flowers in narrow, flat-topped clusters **Blooms:** May to July **Fruits:** egg-shaped, seed-like achenes, with a thick, glandular style on the side; fruits soon shed **Habitat:** dry, open sites **Distribution:** native from Quebec to Alaska to New Mexico **Pick:** a few

Shrubby Cinquefoil

Dasiphora fruticosa

This hardy shrub with its abundant yellow flowers is common in parks and gardens, so travellers may be surprised to see it in the wild. Such plants have not escaped cultivation. Rather, shrubby cinquefoil is a widespread native shrub that has become popular with gardeners. • The stems and leaves were once steeped to make a tea for relieving fevers, coughs and diarrhea. Little evidence supports these medicinal uses, but the tea is considered pleasant and nontoxic. • Some tribes believed that shrubby cinquefoil contained a deadly heart poison, which was applied to arrow tips and porcupine quills for wounding the enemy. • *D. fruticosa* has also been called *Potentilla fruticosa* and *Pentaphylloides floribunda*.

Plant: deciduous shrub 10–100 cm tall, with shredding, reddish brown bark **Leaves:** greyish green, pinnately divided into 3–7 (usually 5) narrowly oblong leaflets 1–2 cm long **Flowers:** saucer-shaped, 1.5–3 cm across, with 5 broad petals, 5 sepals and 5 smaller alternating bractlets; flowers clustered at branch tips **Blooms:** June to September **Fruits:** pale brown, seed-like achenes **Habitat:** open, wet to well-drained sites **Distribution:** native from Newfoundland to Alaska to New Mexico and around the world **Pick:** a few

Prickly Rose
Rosa acicularis

On warm days in summer, these beautiful blossoms—Alberta's floral emblem—emit a delicate fragrance. But beware! The name *acicularis*, 'needle-like,' refers to the abundant protective prickles. • Fragrant rose petals have been used for centuries in potpourris, scented oils and perfumes. In the kitchen, rose flowers make a delicately flavoured tea or can be sprinkled into salads, fruit punches and sandwiches. Outdoors, the petals provide a melt-in-your-mouth nibble likened to perfumed bubblegum. • For centuries, the sweet, red flesh of rose hips has been used for food and as a source of vitamin C. However, the hairy achenes inside can cause 'itchy bottom' and should not be eaten. Rose hips make excellent jelly, syrup, tea and wine and are a valuable winter emergency food.

Plant: prickly deciduous shrub 20–120 cm tall
Leaves: sharply toothed, pinnately divided into 5–7 oblong leaflets 3–4 cm long **Flowers:** pink, saucer-shaped, 5–7 cm across, with 5 petals, 5 slender sepals and numerous stamens; flowers in small, loose clusters on short branches
Blooms: June to August **Fruits:** scarlet hips, berry-like, 1.5–3 cm long, containing hairy, seed-like achenes **Habitat:** dry to moist sites
Distribution: native from Quebec to Alaska to the central U.S.; also Eurasia **Pick:** a few; caution

Virginia Strawberry

Fragaria virginiana

Although its delicate blooms are easily overlooked, Virginia strawberry is one of our commonest wildflowers. Most people know this little plant for its fruits rather than its flowers. Wild strawberries may be small, but each one packs all the flavour of a larger domestic strawberry. • A tea made from strawberry leaves provides a refreshing drink that is rich in vitamin C and minerals. For centuries, it has been used as a safe (but not necessarily effective) remedy for everything from insanity to tuberculosis. This tea is still widely used to treat diarrhea and skin problems. If you decide to try strawberry-leaf tea, use only fresh or completely dried leaves, because the wilted leaves contain toxins. • Virginia strawberry has also been called smooth wild strawberry.

Plant: low perennial, often with slender runners **Leaves:** basal, long-stalked, with 3 coarsely toothed leaflets each tipped with a relatively small tooth **Flowers:** white, 5-petalled, saucer-shaped, 1.5–2 cm across; in small clusters **Blooms:** April to June **Fruits:** strawberries, with tiny, seed-like achenes in pits on the surface of a round, red, fleshy, 1–1.5 cm sphere **Habitat:** dry to moist, sunny to shaded, often disturbed sites **Distribution:** native across North America **Pick:** a few (flowers or fruits)

Northern Crane's-Bill

Geranium bicknellii

These delicate flowers produce narrow, pointed capsules that look like slender beaks, hence the name crane's-bill. When the capsules mature, they split open from bottom to top, releasing seeds in all directions. Five curled strips remain attached at the tip, like upcurved arms on a fairy candelabra. • Astringent crane's-bill roots have been used in gargles for mouth and throat sores, in teas for diarrhea and internal bleeding, and in washes for sores and wounds. • Red-stem stork's-bill *(Erodium cicutarium)*, a noxious European weed, can be confused with northern crane's-bill. Stork's-bill is distinguished by its pinnately divided (not palmate) leaves and by its spirally coiled (not simply upcurved) capsule segments.

Plant: erect to sprawling annual or biennial 10–60 cm tall, freely branched, from slender taproot
Leaves: roughly 5-sided, 2–7 cm across, deeply cut into 5 toothed, wedge-shaped segments arranged like fingers on a hand **Flowers:** pink to rose purple, about 1 cm across, with 5 notched petals and 5 sepals; flowers paired, on slender, glandular-hairy stalks **Blooms:** May to August **Fruits:** cylindrical capsules about 2 cm long, tapered to a beak 4–6 mm long **Habitat:** open, often disturbed sites **Distribution:** native from Newfoundland to Alaska to Tennessee and California **Pick:** a few

Wild Blue Flax

Linum lewisii

Through the years, wild flax has been widely used for food and fibre. As food, flax seeds were usually roasted and ground. Roasting breaks down the small amounts of hydrocyanic acid in raw seeds, making them safe to eat in quantity, and grinding increases the available fibre and releases valuable oils. The strong stem fibres were used to make thread, cord, fishing nets and even snowshoe webbing. • Enjoy this beautiful wildflower where it grows; the delicate blooms wilt within minutes of picking. On each stem, a single flower opens in the morning and closes by late afternoon. The following day, the next bloom opens, and the developing seed capsule of the previous flower begins to enlarge. • This species has also been called prairie flax, Lewis wild flax and *L. perenne*.

Plant: grey-green, hairless perennial 20–70 cm tall, with erect, slender stems from a branched, woody rootstock **Leaves:** many, slender, mostly 1-nerved, 1–2.5 cm long **Flowers:** pale blue to sky blue (rarely white), broadly funnel-shaped, about 2–3.5 cm across, with 5 fragile petals and 5 hairless sepals; flowers borne on arched branches, in open clusters **Blooms:** May to August **Fruits:** round capsules 5–9 mm across, on curved stalks **Habitat:** dry, open sites **Distribution:** native from Ontario to Alaska, south through the U.S. **Pick:** a few

Purple Loosestrife

Lythrum salicaria

Purple loosestrife was introduced to North America in the 1800s as a showy, hardy, disease-resistant garden flower. Today, its brilliant, purplish pink flowers smother wetlands across the continent. The garden varieties were thought sterile (incapable of producing seed), but they soon proved to be decidedly otherwise. One plant can produce more than 2 million seeds, and plants also grow quickly from creeping rootstocks and from root or stem fragments. This aggressive weed has been called 'the silent killer' because few local animals can eat its acrid leaves, tiny seeds and tough roots. Consequently, purple loosestrife thrives unmolested. It rapidly chokes out native plants, converting complex wetland ecosystems into silent monocultures that are largely unpopulated by insects, birds and frogs.

Plant: stout perennial 50–150 cm tall, from spreading rootstock **Leaves:** paired or in threes, 3–10 cm long, stalkless, sometimes clasping the stem **Flowers:** red-purple, 1–2 cm across, usually with 6 wrinkled petals, 6 sepals (sometimes 4) and twice as many, alternately long and short stamens; many flowers in leafy-bracted, branched, spike-like clusters 10–40 cm long **Blooms:** July to August **Fruits:** small capsules **Habitat:** wet sites **Distribution:** Europe; naturalized across temperate North America **Pick:** freely

Common Fireweed

Chamerion angustifolium

Common fireweed will usually form small colonies along roads, but after fires it can blanket charred landscapes with a sea of rose purple flowers. The sweet blooms provide a tasty nibble, a pretty salad garnish and abundant nectar for golden fireweed honey. Tender young plants (under 20 cm tall) have been likened to asparagus and eaten in the same way. Around the world, people drink fireweed tea and cook the leaves as a potherb. Like any new food, it should be introduced slowly; the uninitiated may find fireweed quite laxative. • Older fireweed stems have been split lengthwise to scrape out the soft, edible centre (pith) and to prepare the tough stem fibres for making twine and fishnets. • *C. angustifolium* is also known as *Epilobium angustifolium*.

Plant: erect perennial 50–300 cm tall, from spreading rootstock **Leaves:** many, alternate, lance-shaped **Flowers:** purplish pink (rarely white), about 2.5 cm across, with 4 slender-based petals, 4 sepals, 8 stamens and a cross-shaped stigma; flowers in spike-like clusters
Blooms: June to September
Fruits: slender 3–8 cm pods, splitting lengthwise to release tiny seeds with silky parachutes **Habitat:** highly variable, often disturbed **Distribution:** native across North America and around the world **Pick:** a few

Common Evening-Primrose

Oenothera biennis

Each evening a single delicate flower of common evening-primrose unfurls, releasing its perfume to attract night-flying moths. By noon the following day, the bloom has faded, but if it was pollinated by a moth, its seeds have already started to develop. Each plant usually produces about 6000 oil-rich seeds. North American farmers harvest hundreds of tonnes of evening-primrose seeds each year. The oil from these seeds contains fatty acids that the human body needs in order to produce important hormones. Studies have shown that evening-primrose oil can help treat eczema, asthma, migraine headaches, heart disease, high cholesterol, inflammation, PMS, breast problems, multiple sclerosis, diabetes, rheumatoid arthritis and even alcoholism.

Plant: erect biennial (usually), 50–150 cm tall **Leaves:** lance-shaped to oblong, mostly 10–20 cm long, smooth or wavy-edged **Flowers:** yellow, 2.5–5 cm across, with a long tube (containing the ovary) below 4 petals, 4 sepals, 8 stamens and a protruding style tipped with a cross-shaped stigma; flowers in stiff, leafy-bracted spikes **Blooms:** July to September **Fruits:** erect, persistent, oblong capsules 1.5–4 cm long
Habitat: disturbed ground
Distribution: native across southern Canada and most of the U.S.
Pick: a few

Scarlet Butterflyweed

Gaura coccinea

This beautiful wildflower is often overlooked because its blossoms open just a few at a time. The common name and the epithet *coccinea*, 'scarlet,' refer to the colour of the mature flowers, but when the delicate blooms first open they are not red at all. Instead, the unfolding petals are white. They soon take on pinkish tones, and within a few hours the entire flower has turned a brilliant scarlet. • Scarlet butterflyweed is rare in gardens, but it can be grown from stem cuttings and rootstock divisions. • The paired, spreading petals have been likened to butterfly wings, hence the name butterflyweed. Another common name, scarlet beeblossom, suggests that bees frequently visit these plants in search of pollen and nectar.

Plant: clumped, finely grey-hairy perennial 10–40 cm tall, with sprawling to erect, branched stems **Leaves:** numerous, slender to oblong, 1–3 cm long, with smooth to shallowly toothed edges, stalkless **Flowers:** pale scarlet to brick red, cross-shaped, about 1 cm across, with 4 spoon-shaped petals and 8 large, reddish anthers above a long, reddish tube of 4 sepals; flowers in narrow clusters 5–15 cm long **Blooms:** July to August **Fruits:** finely grey-hairy, 1–4-seeded, 4-sided, nut-like capsules about 6 mm long **Habitat:** dry, open sites **Distribution:** native from Ontario to B.C. to Texas; noxious weed in California **Pick:** a few

Rusty Labrador-Tea

Ledum groenlandicum

This aromatic plant was once used as insect and rodent repellent, but today it is known for its use in making a sweet, fragrant tea. Many aboriginal names are variations of the English word 'tea,' suggesting this use was introduced by Europeans. • In large quantities, Labrador-tea leaves can cause headaches, delirium, palpitations and paralysis, and boiling releases even more toxins. The tea, though, seems to have variable effects. Some people become drowsy, others feel no change and still others report a caffeine-like effect. This beverage should be introduced cautiously, never boiled and always used in moderation. • Rust-coloured hairs on the leaf undersides distinguish Labrador-tea from its poisonous relatives: mountain laurel *(Kalmia)* and bog rosemary *(Andromeda)* have hairless, whitish lower leaf surfaces. • *L. groenlandicum* has also been called *L. palustre* var. *latifolium*.

Plant: evergreen shrub 30–80 cm tall, in colonies from spreading rootstock
Leaves: leathery, deep green, rusty-hairy underneath, oblong, 1–5 cm long, with down-rolled edges **Flowers:** white, about 1 cm across, on long, white-hairy stalks; flowers in rounded clusters at branch tips
Blooms: June to July **Fruits:** nodding, 5-parted capsules 5–7 mm long
Habitat: bogs to moderately dry sites
Distribution: native from Newfoundland to Alaska to the northern U.S.; Greenland
Pick: a few

Showy Milkweed
Asclepias speciosa

When insects visit the fragrant, nectar-rich flowers of showy milkweed, their feet slip under little saddlebags of pollen, which they must pull out and carry in order to fly away. Sometimes smaller insects cannot free their feet and remain trapped on the flower. The strong, sweet perfume of milkweeds makes some people drowsy, and it may also have a stupefying effect on insect visitors. • Showy milkweed is poisonous raw, but the young shoots, leaves and seed pods are all edible cooked. When placed in cold water, brought to a boil and simmered until tender (preferably with a change of water), these parts are said to be delicately flavoured and harmless. The flower buds, nectar-sweet blooms and seeds are also edible.

Plant: erect perennial 30–100 cm tall, with milky sap; usually in colonies from spreading rootstock **Leaves:** paired, broadly oval, 7–15 cm long
Flowers: flesh-toned to greenish purple, 8–12 mm across, with 5 backward-pointing petals around a crown of 5 long, pointed hoods, each with a short, incurved horn; flowers on woolly stalks in round, 5–7 cm clusters **Blooms:** June to August
Fruits: paired, lance-shaped follicles 6–10 cm long, white-woolly and with soft protuberances, releasing silky-parachuted seeds **Habitat:** moist, open sites
Distribution: native from Manitoba to B.C., south through the U.S. **Pick:** a few; caution (irritating sap)

Common Milkweed

Asclepias syriaca

Common milkweed colonies produce impressive networks of rope-like runners about 15 cm underground. Each year, a plant can send up dozens of shoots from these runners. • Milkweeds' milky white sap contains bitter chemicals that help protect these plants from predators. A few lucky insects are immune to these poisons. They feast on milkweed and keep the bitter toxins for their own protection. Monarch butterfly caterpillars eat only milkweed. • *Syriaca* means 'of Syria.' This species was common in southern Europe, so people thought it came from there, but in fact early explorers brought it from North America long before it was officially named. • Common milkweed has also been called silky milkweed.

Plant: perennial 50–150 cm tall
Leaves: paired, thick, soft-hairy underneath, oblong with rounded bases, 10–20 cm long **Flowers:** 8–12 mm across, with 5 backward-pointing, purplish to greenish petals below a crown of 5 pale purple hoods, each with an upcurved horn; flowers in rounded, umbrella-like clusters **Blooms:** June to August **Fruits:** paired, woolly follicles 7–12 cm long, with soft protuberances, releasing silky-parachuted seeds
Habitat: open, disturbed sites
Distribution: native from Quebec to Saskatchewan, south through the U.S.
Pick: freely; caution (irritating sap)

Spreading Dogbane
Apocynum androsaemifolium

Danger lurks in these delicate bells. Each flower conceals five nectaries inside five V-shaped openings edged with tiny teeth. Insects, drawn to the fragrant nectar, often catch their feet in these openings and cannot escape. Fortunately, bees and butterflies are strong enough to free themselves and carry pollen to other flowers. • Women of some tribes rolled dogbane stem fibres on their legs to make thread. It was used for sewing and for making twine, nets, fabric and bowstrings. The poisonous, acrid sap was said to stimulate hair growth by irritating the follicles, but people with sensitive skin are more likely to develop blisters than hair.

Plant: erect, blue-green perennial 20–100 cm tall, usually bushy, with milky sap
Leaves: paired, 3–10 cm long, often drooping
Flowers: pinkish, bell-shaped, 6–10 mm across, with 5 spreading lobes; flowers nodding on slender stalks in branched clusters
Blooms: June to August **Fruits:** hanging, paired, slender follicles 5–15 cm long, splitting to release seeds with silky-white parachutes **Habitat:** sunny, well-drained sites
Distribution: native from Newfoundland to Alaska to southern U.S. **Pick:** freely; caution

Common Viper's-Bugloss

Echium vulgare

Common viper's-bugloss was introduced to North America as a garden flower in the 1600s; by the mid-1800s, agriculturalists were condemning it as a vile foreign weed. Although it is said to be edible, it would make a rather bristly dish. In fact, some people get rashes by simply touching this hairy plant. The beautiful flowers, on the other hand, make a pretty garnish when floated in punch or tossed in salads. • At one time, common viper's-bugloss was said to have the power to drive away sadness, especially when combined with wine. It was also believed to counteract viper venom, and therefore to cure all snake bites. Unfortunately, it was most effective when administered before the bite, which required a certain amount of foresight.

Plant: rough-hairy biennial 30–80 cm tall, from taproot **Leaves:** oblong to lance-shaped, 6–25 cm long, smaller upwards **Flowers:** bright blue to purple (buds pink), asymmetrically funnel-shaped, 1.2–2 cm across, with 4 reddish stamens and a slender style projecting from the mouth; many flowers in elongating clusters with uncoiling, 1-sided branches **Blooms:** June to August **Fruits:** 4 small, rough nutlets **Habitat:** disturbed sites **Distribution:** Europe and north Africa; naturalized from Newfoundland to B.C., Alaska and Texas **Pick:** freely; caution

Tall Bluebells

Mertensia paniculata

If you take a close look at these flower clusters, you'll see that not all of the bells are blue. Flowers that have been pollinated and young buds turn pinkish, whereas mature blooms, ready for pollination, turn blue. Many insects are attracted to blue but can't see red or pink, so they fly to the receptive blue flowers and don't bother with the pink ones. The hanging, bell-shaped corolla shelters the reproductive parts and discourages visits from many insects too small to pollinate the flower but still capable of stealing valuable nectar and pollen. • This hardy, shade-tolerant plant, with its attractive blue bells, makes a lovely addition to wildflower gardens. The large basal leaves were sometimes dried, crushed and smoked, often mixed with tobacco. • Tall bluebells has also been called tall lungwort.

Plant: rough-hairy perennial 30–100 cm tall **Leaves:** coarse, stiff-hairy, 5–14 cm long, heart-shaped at the stem base, progressively narrower and shorter-stalked upwards **Flowers:** blue (fading to pink or white), 1–1.5 cm long, funnel-shaped; corolla with a tubular base and flaring, 5-lobed mouth; calyx hairy, with 5 slender lobes; flowers nodding, in elongating clusters **Blooms:** June to August **Fruits:** 4 wrinkled nutlets **Habitat:** moist, often wooded sites **Distribution:** native across Canada, south to the northern U.S. **Pick:** a few

Harebell

Campanula rotundifolia

This delicate, nodding wild-flower is the famous bluebell of Scotland. Although harebell is a hardy, resilient plant, it is also the essence of fragility, with its graceful blue bells bobbing on hair-like stems. Small insects find it difficult to crawl inside these flowers to steal pollen and nectar, but bees and other flying pollina-tors have easy access. • The nod-ding bells trap warm air and protect styles and stamens from rain. Mature capsules sway back and forth on slender elastic stalks, scattering seeds from holes in their sides like swinging salt shakers. • The epithet for this species, *rotundifolia*, refers to the rounded leaves at the bottom of the plant. These basal leaves have usually withered away by the time the flowers open, and only the slender stem leaves remain.

Plant: slender perennial 10–80 cm tall
Leaves: mainly on stem, slender, stalk-less, 1.5–8 cm long; rounded, stalked basal leaves also present but soon fade
Flowers: blue, bell-shaped, 5-lobed, 1.5–2.5 cm long; 1 to many nodding on thread-like stalks in loose, elongating clusters **Blooms:** June to September
Fruits: nodding capsules, opening by pores on the sides near the base
Habitat: well-drained, often rocky sites
Distribution: native across North Amer-ica south to Mexico, and around the world **Pick:** a few

Field Bindweed

Convolvulus arvensis

This small, twining plant bears charming, morning-glory-like flowers. Unfortunately, it can soon become a most troublesome weed, clambering over other plants in a smothering blanket. The genus name comes from the Latin word *convolvere*, 'to entwine.' Field bindweed's tendrils wind tightly around any slender support nearby and can complete a 360° twist every 100 minutes. • Although each plant is capable of producing more than 500 long-lived seeds, field bindweed seldom fruits. Instead, plants usually reproduce by vegetative means. Rootstocks can stretch 4 m, sending up new shoots along the way. When broken, even small pieces of these deep, brittle runners can become new plants. Newly established bindweed plants also release toxins into the soil to poison other species and reduce competition for water, nutrients and sunlight.

Plant: slender, trailing or climbing perennial, with 30–100 cm stems from deep, spreading rootstock **Leaves:** triangular to arrowhead-shaped, 2–5 cm long **Flowers:** white to pink, broadly funnel-shaped, 1.5–2.5 cm across, twisted in bud; flowers single or paired on long stalks from leaf axils **Blooms:** May to September **Fruits:** small, cone-shaped capsules, usually hanging **Habitat:** disturbed ground **Distribution:** Europe; naturalized across southern Canada and throughout the U.S. **Pick:** freely

Hedge False-Bindweed

Calystegia sepium

The name *Calystegia*, 'beautiful covering,' refers to the two leafy bracts that enclose the bud and later cover the base of this flower. The name could as easily refer to this plant's lovely lush mats of triangular leaves, which are dotted with showy, white to pinkish flowers. Each twisted flower bud unwinds into a broad funnel during the day, retwisting at night and when it has finished blooming. Pink or white lines (nectar guides) inside the funnel lead insects to five nectar-containing pits at the bottom.
• Although hedge false-bindweed can be a serious weed, it produces striking flowered blankets when allowed to trail over walls and fences. Several European forms have been introduced as garden plants, and today both native and introduced forms grow wild across much of North America.
• *C. sepium* has also been called *Convolvulus sepium*.

Plant: climbing or trailing perennial, with 1–3 m stems from spreading rootstock
Leaves: arrowhead-shaped, 5–12 cm long **Flowers:** white to pink, broadly funnel-shaped, 4–7 cm across, with 5 sepals enclosed by 2 heart-shaped, 1–2 cm bracts; flowers long-stalked, single in leaf axils **Blooms:** May to September
Fruits: cone-shaped capsules, usually hanging **Habitat:** moist, often disturbed sites **Distribution:** native in temperate North America and Eurasia **Pick:** freely

Page numbers indicate where terms are illustrated.

achene: a small, dry fruit that doesn't split open when mature, often seed-like in appearance, distinguished from a nutlet by its relatively thin wall (pp. 12, 150)

alternate: situated singly at each joint or node (e.g., as leaves on a stem) or regularly between other organs (e.g., as stamens alternate with petals) (p. 148)

annual: a plant that completes its life cycle in 1 growing season

anther: the pollen-bearing part of a stamen (pp. 11, 12)

ascending: growing upwards on an angle

axil: the angle between a side organ (e.g., a leaf) and the part to which it is attached (e.g., a stem) (p. 148)

basal: located at the base or arising from it, e.g., leaves at the base of a stem (p. 148)

beak: a prolonged, more or less slender tip on a thicker organ such as a fruit (p. 150)

berry: a fleshy fruit, usually with several to many seeds

biennial: living for 2 years, usually producing flowers and seed in the 2nd year

bilaterally symmetrical: divisible into 2 equal parts along 1 line only (p. 18); compare 'radially symmetrical'

blade: the broad, flat part of a leaf or petal (p. 148)

bract: a specialized leaf with a flower (or sometimes a flower cluster) arising from its axil (pp. 12, 150)

bulb: a fleshy underground organ with overlapping, swollen scales, e.g., an onion

calyx: the sepals of a flower, collectively (p. 11)

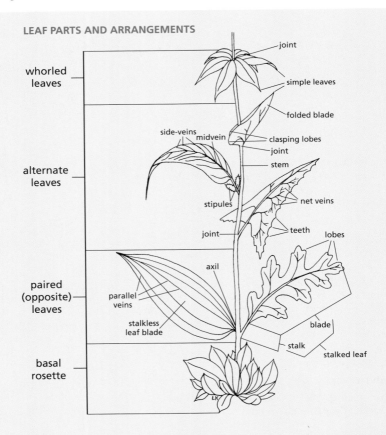

LEAF PARTS AND ARRANGEMENTS

whorled leaves

alternate leaves

paired (opposite) leaves

basal rosette

joint
simple leaves
folded blade
side-veins
midvein
clasping lobes
joint
stem
net veins
stipules
joint
teeth
lobes
axil
parallel veins
stalkless leaf blade
blade
stalk
stalked leaf

capsule: a dry fruit that splits open when mature, often with more than 1 seed (p. 150)

chambered: with inner cavities

circumpolar: found in northern areas around the world

clambering: sprawling and trailing over the ground

clasping: embracing or surrounding, usually in reference to a leaf base around a stem (p. 148)

compound: divided into smaller parts (p. 149)

corolla: the petals of a flower, collectively (p. 11)

creeping: growing along (or beneath) the surface of the ground and producing roots and sometimes shoots at intervals (usually at joints)

crown: the part of a plant where the stems and roots meet

cultivar: a cultivated variety, i.e., a plant or animal originating in cultivation

drupe: a fleshy, pulpy, 1-seeded fruit with a stony covering on the seed (p. 150)

elongating cluster: a flower cluster that lengthens as it develops, with flowers and fruits forming at the base first and then upwards to the tip; a raceme (p. 150)

family: a group of related plants or animals forming a category of biological classification above genus, e.g., the aster family (Asteraceae); see p. 154 for a list of all families in this book

fibrous roots: slender, fibre-like roots, usually numerous and clumped

fleshy: plump, firm and pulpy; succulent

floret: a small flower, usually 1 of several in a cluster (pp. 12, 18)

flowerhead: a dense cluster of tiny flowers (florets), often appearing as a single flower; typical of the aster family (pp. 12, 18)

follicle: a dry, pod-like fruit that splits open along a single line on 1 side (p. 150)

fringed: edged with a row of hairs (p. 151)

fruit: a ripened ovary, together with any other structures that develop with it as a unit

genus [genera]: a group of related plants or animals constituting a category of biological classification below family and above species; the first word of a scientific name indicates the genus, e.g., *Achillea* in *Achillea millefolium* (often abbreviated, e.g., *A. millefolium*)

gland: in plants, a small depression, bump or appendage that produces a thick, sticky or greasy fluid

glandular: with glands

herb: a plant that lacks woody above-ground parts and dies back to the ground in winter

COMPOUND-LEAF PARTS

palmately divided
(like fingers on a hand)

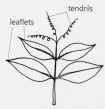

pinnately divided
(like barbs on a feather)

BLADE SHAPES

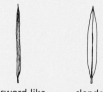

sword-like   slender
(linear)

oblong   lance-shaped

ovate   elliptic

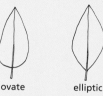

oval   heart-shaped

FLOWER ARRANGEMENTS

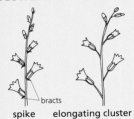

bracts

spike   elongating cluster

leafy
bracts

umbrella-shaped cluster

FRUIT TYPES

silky hairs
(parachute)

stalk-
like
beak

lens-shaped

beak

spiny ribs   wing

achenes

persistent
style

corky ribs

schizocarp

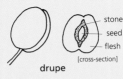

stone

seed

flesh

[cross-section]

drupe

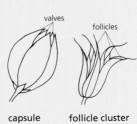

valves

follicles

capsule   follicle cluster

introduced: brought in from another region (e.g., from Europe), not native; such exotic plants often lack predators and other population controls present in the native range

keel: the two partly united lower petals of a pea-like flower (p. 152)

latex: milky plant juice containing rubbery compounds

leaflet: a single segment of a compound leaf (p. 149)

lens-shaped: discus-shaped, with 2 regular opposite sides either both curved or 1 curved and 1 flat (p. 150)

lip: a projection or expansion of a structure, such as the lower petal of a flower (p. 152)

lobe: a rounded or strap-shaped division of a leaf, petal or other structure (pp. 148, 151)

monoculture: a growth of only 1 kind of organism (e.g., 1 species of plant) in an area

mucilage: a sticky, gelatinous plant substance

mycorrhiza [mycorrhizae]: the mutually beneficial (symbiotic) association of certain fungi with the roots of certain seed plants

native: originating in a place (e.g., Manitoba); indigenous

naturalized: originating in a distant region; introduced and growing wild in a new region

nerved: with prominent longitudinal lines or veins

noxious weed: an aggressive, usually introduced plant that rapidly invades sites where it is not wanted; in the legal sense, an invasive plant species requiring management or control because of legislative action

nutlet: a small, hard, dry, 1-seeded fruit or part of a fruit, not splitting open when mature

ovary: the structure at the base of a pistil that contains the young, undeveloped seeds (ovules) (p. 11)

palmate: divided into 3 or more lobes or leaflets that diverge from 1 point, like fingers on a hand (p. 149)

perennial: living for 3 or more years

persistent: remaining attached long after normal function has been completed

petal: a member of the inside ring of modified flower leaves, usually brightly coloured or white (pp. 11, 12)

pinnate: with parts (branches, lobes, leaflets, veins) arranged on both sides of a central stalk or vein, like the barbs of a feather; feather-like (p. 149)

pistil: the female organ of a flower, usually consisting of an ovary, style and stigma (p. 11)

pod: a dry fruit that splits open to release its seeds

pollen: the powdery contents of an anther, each grain containing male cells

pollinate: to transfer pollen from an anther to a stigma

pollination: the process of pollinating

prolific: producing many offspring

radially symmetrical: with parts arranged like spokes on a wheel, therefore divisible into equal parts along 2 or more lines (p. 19); compare 'bilaterally symmetrical'

rootstock: an underground, usually lengthened stem, distinguished from a true root by the presence of joints (nodes) and buds or scale-like leaves; a rhizome

rosette: a cluster of crowded, usually basal leaves in a circular arrangement (p. 148)

runner: a slender, horizontally spreading stem that often roots at its joints and tips

scale: any small, thin, flat structure

schizocarp: a dry fruit that splits into 2 or more parts when mature, e.g., fruits of the carrot family (p. 150)

sepal: a member of the outer ring of modified flower leaves, usually green and more or less leafy in texture but sometimes colourful (p. 11)

sheathing: partly or wholly surrounding another organ

simple: undivided (p. 148)

species (*abbrev.* sp.) [species, spp.]: a group of closely related plants or animals; the fundamental unit of biological classification, indicated by the second word of a scientific name (the specific epithet), e.g., *millefolium* in *Achillea millefolium*

specific epithet: see 'species'

spike: a simple, unbranched flower cluster, with (essentially) stalkless flowers arranged on an elongated main stalk (p. 150)

spindle-shaped: cylindrical and tapered to a point at both ends

spreading: diverging from the vertical, approaching horizontal

spur: a hollow appendage on a petal or sepal, usually functioning as a nectar gland (p. 152)

stamen: the pollen-bearing (male) organ of a flower consisting of an anther and a filament (p. 11)

sterile: incapable of producing seed

stigma: the tip of the female organ (pistil), where the pollen lands (pp. 11, 12)

stipules: a pair of bract-like or leaf-like appendages at the base of a leaf stalk (p. 148)

strap-like floret: a small, often showy flower (floret) with a narrow, ribbon-like strap of fused petals, in a flowerhead of the aster family; a ray floret (p. 12)

LEAF BLADE EDGES

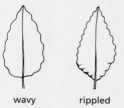

wavy   rippled

toothed   sharp-toothed

spiny-toothed   fringed

finely blunt-toothed   irregularly coarse-toothed

shallowly lobed   deeply lobed

FLOWER SHAPES

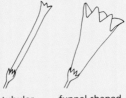

tubular   funnel-shaped

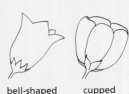

bell-shaped   cupped

saucer-shaped

cross-shaped (4-petalled)

keel

wings

pea-like

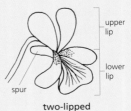

upper lip

lower lip

spur

two-lipped

style: the part of the pistil connecting the stigma to the ovary, often elongated and stalk-like (pp. 11, 150)

subspecies (*abbrev.* ssp.): a group of closely related plants or animals within a species, ranked below species and above variety in biological classification

taproot: a root system with a prominent main root, directed vertically downwards and bearing smaller side-roots, sometimes becoming very swollen and containing stored food material (starch or sugar), e.g., a carrot

tendril: a slender, clasping or twining outgrowth from a stem or leaf (p. 149)

tepal: a sepal or petal, when these structures are not easily distinguished

tooth: a small, often pointed lobe on the edge of a plant part (usually on a leaf) (pp. 148, 151)

trailing: spreading flat on the ground but not rooting

tuber: a thickened portion of a below-ground stem or root, serving for food storage and often also for propagation; e.g., a potato is a stem tuber

tubular floret: a small, tubular flower (floret) with fused petals, in a flowerhead of the aster family; a disc floret (p. 12)

umbrella-shaped cluster: a branched flower grouping in which the branches radiate from 1 joint and curve upwards like the ribs of an umbrella to produce a flat-topped to rounded cluster; an umbel (p. 150)

variety (*abbrev.* var.): a group of similar variants of a species, ranked below subspecies in biological classification

vegetative reproduction: producing new plants from asexual parts (e.g., rootstocks, leaves, stem fragments); the offspring are genetically identical to (i.e., clones of) the parent plant

vein: a strand of conducting tubes (i.e., a vascular bundle containing phloem and xylem), especially if visible externally, as in a leaf (p. 148)

weed: a common, undesirable or troublesome plant that grows in abundance, especially on cultivated or waste ground; many of our weeds have been introduced from Eurasia; see also 'noxious weed'

whorl: a ring of 3 or more similar structures (e.g., leaves, branches or flowers) arising from 1 joint or node (p. 148)

wing: a thin, flattened expansion on the side(s) or tip of a plant part, e.g., on a seed or a stalk (p. 150); also, 1 of the 2 side-petals of a pea-like flower (p. 152)

winged: with 1 or more wings

winter-annual: a plant that grows from seed in late summer or fall, overwinters as a small plant and then flowers, fruits and dies the following spring or summer

Bubar, C. J., S. J. McColl et al. (2000). *Weeds of the Prairies*. Edmonton, Alberta Agriculture, Food and Rural Development.

Budd, A. C. (1957). *Wild Plants of the Canadian Prairies*. Ottawa, Canada Department of Agriculture.

Carmichael, L. T. (1961). *Prairie Wildflowers*. Toronto, J. M. Dent and Sons.

Coffey, T. (1993). *The History and Folklore of North American Wildflowers*. New York, Facts on File.

Couplan, F. (1998). *The Encyclopedia of Edible Plants of North America*. New Canaan, Keats Publishing.

Currah, R., A. Smreciu et al. (1983). *Prairie Wildflowers*. Edmonton, Friends of the Devonian Botanic Garden, University of Alberta.

Erichsen-Brown, C. (1979). *Use of Plants for the Past 500 Years*. Aurora, Breezy Creeks Press.

Foster, S. and J. A. Duke (1990). *Field Guide to Medicinal Plants: Eastern and Central North America*. Boston, Houghton Mifflin Company.

Grieve, M. (1931). *A Modern Herbal*. Harmondsworth, England, Jonathan Cape. Republished in 1976 by Penguin Books.

Johnson, D., L. Kershaw et al. (1995). *Plants of the Western Boreal Forest and Aspen Parkland*. Edmonton, Lone Pine Publishing.

Kershaw, L. (2000). *Edible and Medicinal Plants of the Rockies*. Edmonton, Lone Pine Publishing.

Looman, J. and K. F. Best (1979). *Budd's Flora of the Canadian Prairie Provinces*. Hull, Canadian Government Publishing Centre.

Marles, R. L., C. Clavelle et al. (2000). *Aboriginal Plant Use in Canada's Northwest Boreal Forest*. Vancouver, UBC Press.

Mulligan, G. A. and D. B. Munro (1990). *Poisonous Plants of Canada*. Ottawa, Agriculture Canada.

Niering, W. A. and N. C. Olmstead (1979). *National Audubon Society Field Guide to North American Wildflowers*. New York, Alfred A. Knopf.

Peirce, A. (1999). *The American Pharmaceutical Association Practical Guide to Natural Medicines*. New York, William Morrow and Company.

Peterson, L. A. (1977). *A Field Guide to Edible Wild Plants of Eastern and Central North America*. Boston, Houghton Mifflin Company.

Pond, B. (1974). *A Sampler of Wayside Herbs: Discovering Old Uses for Familiar Wild Plants*. Riverside, Chatham Press.

Reader's Digest (1986). *Magic and Medicine of Plants*. Montreal, The Reader's Digest Association.

Rogers, D. J. (1980). *Edible, Medicinal, Useful, and Poisonous Wild Plants of the Northern Great Plains–South Dakota Region*. Sioux Falls, Biology Department, Augustana College.

Royer, F. and R. Dickinson (1998). *Weeds of Canada and the Northern United States: A Guide for Identification*. Edmonton, University of Alberta Press.

Scoggan, H. G. (1957). *Flora of Manitoba*. National Museum of Canada, Bulletin No. 140: 1–619.

Stokes, D. and L. Stokes (1985). *A Guide to Enjoying Wildflowers*. Toronto, Little, Brown and Company.

Tilford, G. L. (1997). *Edible and Medicinal Plants of the West*. Missoula, Mountain Press Publishing Company.

Vance, F. R., J. R. Jowsey et al. (1977). *Wildflowers Across the Prairies*. Saskatoon, Western Producer Prairie Books.

Westbrooks, R. G. and J. W. Preacher (1986). *Poisonous Plants of Eastern North America*. Columbia, University of South Carolina Press.

White, D. J., E. Haber et al. (1993). *Invasive Plants of Natural Habitats in Canada*. Ottawa, Canadian Wildlife Service, Environment Canada and the Canadian Museum of Nature.

Common Name	Scientific Name	Page Numbers
Arum Family	Araceae	58
Aster Family	Asteraceae	60–90
Bellflower Family	Campanulaceae	145
Bladderwort Family	Lentibulariaceae	39
Borage Family	Boraginaceae	143–144
Buck-bean Family	Menyanthaceae	108
Buttercup Family	Ranunculaceae	102, 115–118
Caper Family	Capparidaceae	120
Carrot Family	Apiaceae	92–96
Dogbane Family	Apocynaceae	142
Dogwood Family	Cornaceae	59
Evening-primrose Family	Onagraceae	136–138
Figwort Family	Scrophulariaceae	38
Flax Family	Linaceae	134
Fumitory Family	Fumariaceae	37
Geranium Family	Geraniaceae	133
Heath Family	Ericaceae	139
Iris Family	Iridaceae	110
Lily Family	Liliaceae	97, 111–113
Loosestrife Family	Lythraceae	135
Madder Family	Rubiaceae	99–100
Mallow Family	Malvaceae	123
Milkweed Family	Asclepiadaceae	140–141
Mint Family	Lamiaceae	40–42, 101
Morning-glory Family	Convolvulaceae	146–147
Mustard Family	Brassicaceae	104–107
Orchid Family	Orchidaceae	36
Pea Family	Fabaceae	45–56
Pink Family	Caryophyllaceae	121–122
Primrose Family	Primulaceae	124
Rose Family	Rosaceae	125–132
Sandalwood Family	Santalaceae	98
Saxifrage Family	Saxifragaceae	119
Smartweed Family	Polygonaceae	57, 103
Spurge Family	Euphorbiaceae	91
Violet Family	Violaceae	43–44
Water-lily Family	Nymphaeaceae	114
Water-plantain Family	Alismataceae	109

- ❑ Alexanders, heart-leaved
- ❑ alfalfa
- ❑ American-aster, fringed
- ❑ American-aster, smooth blue
- ❑ anemone, Canada
- ❑ arrowhead, arum-leaved
- ❑ avens, three-flowered
- ❑ avens, yellow
- ❑ bedstraw, northern
- ❑ beeplant
- ❑ bergamot, wild
- ❑ bindweed, field
- ❑ bird's-foot-trefoil
- ❑ black-eyed Susan
- ❑ bladderwort, greater
- ❑ blanketflower, great
- ❑ blazingstar, dotted
- ❑ bluebells, tall
- ❑ blue-eyed-grass, common
- ❑ bluets, long-leaved
- ❑ buck-bean
- ❑ bunchberry
- ❑ burdock, lesser
- ❑ butter-and-eggs
- ❑ buttercup, meadow
- ❑ butterflyweed, scarlet
- ❑ calla, water
- ❑ campion, bladder
- ❑ chamomile, scentless
- ❑ cinquefoil, plains
- ❑ cinquefoil, shrubby
- ❑ cinquefoil, white
- ❑ clover, alsike
- ❑ clover, red
- ❑ corydalis, golden
- ❑ cow-parsnip, common
- ❑ crane's-bill, northern
- ❑ daisy, oxeye
- ❑ dandelion, common
- ❑ death-camas, white
- ❑ dock, curly
- ❑ dogbane, spreading
- ❑ evening-primrose, common
- ❑ false-bindweed, hedge
- ❑ false-golden-aster, hairy
- ❑ false-Solomon's-seal, starry
- ❑ false-toadflax
- ❑ fireweed, common
- ❑ flax, wild blue
- ❑ fleabane, Philadelphia
- ❑ fleabane, smooth
- ❑ giant-hyssop, blue
- ❑ globe-mallow, scarlet
- ❑ goat's-beard, common
- ❑ goldenrod, Canada
- ❑ grass-of-Parnassus, northern
- ❑ gumweed, curly-cup
- ❑ harebell
- ❑ hawk's-beard, annual
- ❑ hawkweed, narrow-leaved
- ❑ hawkweed, orange
- ❑ hedge-nettle, hairy
- ❑ hemp-nettle, brittle-stem
- ❑ Joe-Pye weed, spotted
- ❑ Labrador-tea, rusty
- ❑ lady's-slipper, yellow
- ❑ lettuce, common blue
- ❑ lettuce, prickly
- ❑ licorice, American
- ❑ lily, wood
- ❑ locoweed, late yellow
- ❑ locoweed, showy
- ❑ loosestrife, purple
- ❑ marsh-marigold, yellow
- ❑ meadow-rue, tall
- ❑ milkweed, common
- ❑ milkweed, showy
- ❑ mouse-ear-chickweed, field
- ❑ mustard, tumbleweed
- ❑ mustard, wild
- ❑ onion, prairie
- ❑ parsnip, wild
- ❑ pepper-grass, common
- ❑ pineappleweed
- ❑ plumeless-thistle, nodding
- ❑ pond-lily, yellow
- ❑ prairie-crocus
- ❑ pussytoes, little-leaved
- ❑ ragwort, marsh
- ❑ rose, prickly
- ❑ silverweed, common
- ❑ smartweed, water
- ❑ sow-thistle, perennial
- ❑ spurge, leafy
- ❑ strawberry, Virginia
- ❑ sunflower, annual
- ❑ sweet-clover
- ❑ sweet-colt's-foot, arctic
- ❑ sweet-vetch, American
- ❑ tansy, common
- ❑ thistle, Canada
- ❑ vetch, American
- ❑ vetchling, cream-coloured
- ❑ vetchling, veiny
- ❑ violet, Canada
- ❑ violet, early blue
- ❑ viper's-bugloss, common
- ❑ wallflower, wormseed
- ❑ water-hemlock, spotted
- ❑ water-parsnip, common
- ❑ yarrow, common
- ❑ yellow-loosestrife, fringed

*A*n avid naturalist since childhood, Linda Kershaw focused on botany at the University of Waterloo, earning her master's degree in 1976. Since then she has worked as a consultant and researcher in northwestern Canada and as an author and editor in Edmonton, while pursuing two favourite pastimes—photography and illustrating. Linda hopes that her books will help people appreciate the beauty and fascinating history of plants and recognize the intrinsic value of nature's rich mosaic. Linda is the author or co-author of 8 Lone Pine field guides, including *Plants of the Western Boreal Forest and Aspen Parkland.*

Over many years in the field with Linda, sons Geoff (left, 16 field seasons) and Eric (21 seasons) and husband Peter (far right, 29 seasons) have travelled thousands of kilometres and developed sharp eyes in the never-ending search for wild plants and animals. They've also learned the virtue of patience as 15-minute walks turn into 2-hour photo sessions. Linda dedicates the wayside wildflower guides to her family, to thank them for their continued patience and support and for many happy hours of hiking through wild and not-so-wild places.